LIBRARIES

THROUGH THE AGES

LIBRARIES

THROUGH THE AGES

· FRED LERNER ·

CONTINUUM ◆ NEW YORK

1999
The Continuum Publishing Company
370 Lexington Avenue
New York, NY 10017

Printed in the United States of America

Library of Congress Cataloging-in-Publication Data

Lerner, Frederick Andrew, 1945–
    Libraries through the ages / Fred Lerner.
        p.   cm.
    Based on the author's The story of libraries.
    Includes bibliographical references (p.   ) and index.
    Summary: A history of libraries throughout the world,
from those of the ancient Sumerians and Egyptians
to the comprehensive libraries of today.
    ISBN 0-8264-1201-7 (alk. paper)
    1. Libraries—History—Juvenile literature. [1. Libraries—
history.]   I. Lerner, Frederick Andrew. 1945–
Story of libraries.   II. Title.
Z721.L564   1999
027'.009—dc21   99–33321
                                                    CIP

To my parents
Ira and Shirley Lerner
who introduced me to the
Mount Vernon Public Library

Contents

8 • *Contents*

List of Illustrations

Preface

People are "time-binding animals," a philosopher once said. We learn things and we imagine things, and we pass these facts and fancies from one generation to another. Our ancestors evolved language to convey our thoughts, and invented writing to record them. And soon after that, our ancestors started libraries, to preserve and organize them.

◆   ◆   ◆

A library is more than a building, more than a mere collection of books. A library is a collection of books assembled for a purpose. That purpose has varied through history—and the library is a social institution as old as history itself.

My purpose in writing this book is to explore the roles of libraries in the societies that gave birth to them. Why did people go to the trouble and expense of collecting and preserving books? Whose interests did libraries serve, and whose did they not serve? How were libraries shaped by the societies in which they arose—and how did they in turn help to shape those societies? Those are the questions that this book attempts to answer.

In writing this book I have drawn upon the work of a great many historians, archaeologists, and other scholars.* As my intention is to tell a story rather than to document every statement of fact, I have not cluttered this book with footnotes. A short list of suggested readings will guide those interested in learning more about the history of books, printing, and libraries. Terms that might be unfamiliar to newcomers to library history are defined in a glossary at the end of the book.

Libraries are the means by which the present learns from the past, and leaves its own intellectual legacy to the future. We are the heirs of five thousand years of learning, and in *Libraries through the Ages* I have tried to trace how that inheritance has come down to us.

Fred Lerner
White River Junction, Vermont,
February 1999

---

* A complete list of my sources may be found at the end of my earlier book, *The Story of Libraries: From the Invention of Writing to the Computer Age*, which traces the history of libraries in greater detail.

· 1 ·

The Fertile Crescent

Five thousand years ago, in the land we now call Iraq, the Sumerians invented writing. Reeds grew abundantly in the Mesopotamian marshes, and by splitting them the Sumerians produced inexpensive writing instruments. When these were pressed into wet clay, they left a wedge-shaped mark. (We call this writing "cuneiform," from the Latin word for wedge.) The Sumerians baked their clay tablets in kilns, or dried them in the sun. Tens of thousands of these tablets have come down to us, to be read, studied, and translated by generations of scholars.

Much of the Sumerian economy was managed by the temples. The temple administrators depended on scribes, educated men who wrote down the details of business transactions and preserved these records in temple storerooms for future use. Besides business records, the temples collected the texts of hymns, prayers, and incantations. These were used in the education of scribes, but also served a more solemn purpose. The welfare of the Sumerian people depended upon the goodwill of the gods. It was essential to assure that praise and petition alike were offered in the prescribed form.

Sumeria's neighbors also kept written records. In the city of Ebla, capital of an empire extending into Palestine and the Phoenecian coast, the royal palace contained a reference library of dictionaries and syllabaries. These were used by scribes editing definitive versions of literary texts. The library's collection included epic narratives, myths, hymns, incantations, rituals, and proverbs, as well as manuals of botany, zoology, mineralogy, and mathematics.

The palace library at Ebla served as a school library for the academy where scribes were trained. Like a modern university, this academy did more than teach. The scholars of Ebla studied the knowledge of the Sumerians, and extended it with knowledge of their own. Scribes and scholars from other countries visited the city, bringing texts from their native lands, and returning with texts from Ebla.

Ebla was not unique. At Mari, a city in what is now northwestern Iraq, and at the Hittite capital of Boghazkoy (Hattusha) in what is now Turkey, archaeologists have discovered similar archives. There are doubtless other sites in the Fertile Crescent, as yet unexcavated, from which we will learn more about the literary culture of the ancient world, and the libraries that preserved it.

* * *

The ancient Egyptians had several uses for writing, and for scribes. They had to keep track of property ownership and tax payments, record the annual floods of the Nile, and extol the exploits of their kings. Trade with other countries was important, so they collected geographical knowledge and glossaries of foreign languages to help their merchants.

The Egyptians revered tradition. The educated Egyptian saw himself as a link in the maintenance of tradition through the ages, and hoped to continue this work in the afterlife. The written word made this possible. "Copy your fathers who were before you," an Egyptian scribe urged his son. "Their words are made lasting in writing."[1]

While the Egyptians used hieroglyphics for inscriptions on pyramids and monuments, most of their documents were written on papyrus, using the hieratic script. This combined hieroglyphics with signs that represented sounds. But unlike our own alphabet, each sign stood for an entire syllable rather than a single vowel or consonant.

Papyrus was made from the stem of a common reed that grew in the marshes of the Nile delta. By gluing sheets of papyrus together, a book could be made as long as its author desired. (Manuscripts up to one hundred twenty-five feet long have survived.) Papyrus rolls were stored in jars or in wooden chests, which made it easy for traveling officials to use them. The title or a description of the contents was written on the blank outer side of the roll, or a small papyrus or parchment label would be pasted to it. Thus it could be identified quickly without being unrolled.

Doctors and lawyers used papyrus rolls in their practice. When Weshptah, King Neferrirrkere's vizier, suffered a stroke, the king had "a case of writings" brought to the patient's bedside. The *Book of Surgery* might have been one of the books in this portable medical library. It describes forty-eight cases and the treatment recommended for them.

One of the vizier's duties was the administration of justice. He was required to render decisions fairly and in accordance with the way things had been done in the past. So he would consult the records of earlier cases to determine the appropriate punishment for a criminal, and examine events far in the past to settle a disputed inheritance or land claim. Each of these documents bore the seals of the judge who decided the case and the scribe who wrote down the decision. After the vizier examined one, he placed his own seal upon it.

The most famous library of ancient Egypt was established thirty-three hundred years ago by Ramesses II. It was part of the Ramesseum, his temple complex at Thebes. Like other Egyptian temples it contained a "House of Life," in which a picture gallery, library, and dining hall awaited the king's pleasure in the afterlife. Above the entrance to this "sacred library" was inscribed the phrase "Healing-place of the Soul." Its contents included both literary and practical works: poetry, fiction, history; agriculture, astronomy, engineering. Even in the days of the great Alexandrian Library, more than a thousand years later, men remembered the sacred library of King Ramesses.

◆ ◆ ◆

When the 19th-century British archaeologist Austen Henry Layard excavated the ruins of the ancient Assyrian capital of Nineveh, he uncovered more than twenty-five thousand clay tablets. They were part of the library of the temple of Nabu, the Assyrian god of wisdom. This library had been built up by several rulers, but it reached its peak in the 7th century B.C.E. under Assurbanipal, the last great king of Assyria.

Assurbanipal was a learned man who enjoyed reading and writing. He sent scribes to schools and libraries throughout his kingdom, and personally edited the texts they collected. After Assyria conquered Babylon, Assurbanipal seized the opportunity to augment his library with tablets confiscated from Babylonian collectors. But he allowed his unwilling contributors to retain those texts essential to the practice of their professions.

Assurbanipal's library was a well-organized operation. It had its own factory for making tablets and its own kiln for baking them, to ensure high quality. These were inscribed carefully in a uniform script, with high standards of accuracy. In size they ranged from less than a square inch to more than a foot long; they were usually rectangular, and an inch thick.

They were arranged in series, so that all material on the same subject was gathered together. Literary works, such as the creation epic *Enuma elish* or the *Epic of Gilgamesh*, might occupy a dozen tablets or less. Mathematical, astrological, or magical collections included as many as a hundred tablets.

The Assyrian scribes were very much interested in the supernatural: predicting the future, averting evil, placating the gods, exorcising demons. Hundreds of "omen texts" recorded objects or events and the predictions derived from them. Each tablet contained between eighty and two hundred short entries. It must have been a difficult task to find the relevant omens from the tens of thousands in the collection. Unusual weather or changes in the night sky provoked queries to the royal astrologers; hundreds of their replies were preserved in the palace library. Spells, charms, prayers, and hymns were preserved in carefully edited versions. And the kings wrote letters reporting their accomplishments to the omnipotent god Ashur. Though these were sealed within the library, the kings were confident that Ashur would be able to read them.

For us, the most significant documents preserved in Assurbanipal's library were the legends of a great flood, known to us today as the *Epic of Gilgamesh*. These legends were collected from older Sumerian texts, and may have their origins fifteen hundred years before the time of Assurbanipal. This would make them older than the poems of Homer or the Bible.

There are hints that a version of the Gilgamesh story might have been known to the early authors of the books of the Bible. "Written down according to the original and collated in the palace of Assurbanipal, King of the World, King of Assyria,"[2] they have come down to us.

It is fortunate that they did. Fifteen years after Assurbanipal's death, the Medes and Babylonians so completely destroyed Nineveh that it was never rebuilt, and Assurbanipal's great library was buried beneath the rubble of the city.

· · ·

"The making of many books is without limit, And much study is a wearying of the flesh."[3] So the book of Ecclesiastes tells us; and for thousands of years many people have wearied their flesh in studying the Bible.

The Hebrew Bible is a collection of texts considered to be sacred, selected by agreement of priests and rabbis for preservation, study, and liturgical use. This canonization process took hundreds of years, beginning in the Babylonian exile (6th century B.C.E.) and reaching completion only in the 2nd century C.E. There must have been a considerable body of literature from which works were chosen. Throughout the Bible we find the names of other books that no longer exist, such as the *Book of the Wars of the Lord* quoted in Numbers 21:14 and the *Chronicles of the Kings of Israel* and *Chronicles of the Kings of Judah* cited frequently in I and II Kings. There were probably others whose names we do not even know.

We know very little about how this literature was preserved and made available to those selecting the books that became part of the Bible. But from clues contained within the Bible itself we can make some educated guesses. In Deuteronomy we are told that Moses ordered the Levites to "take this book of

Teaching and place it beside the Ark of the Covenant of the Lord your God, and let it remain there as a witness against you."[4] Centuries later, the priest Samuel recorded the rules of the Israelite monarchy "in a document which he deposited before the Lord."[5]

The holy books were kept in holy places: the Ark of the Covenant, the tabernacle at Shiloh, the Temple in Jerusalem. They were written on animal skins, which were readily available to a pastoral people. We do not know how they were stored and retrieved for use. One possibility is that scrolls were kept in clay jars, which were used to preserve important legal records. In the caves of Qumran, the Dead Sea Scrolls were stored this way. Priestly families or scribal schools may have stored their books in wooden or metal chests fashioned after the Ark of the Covenant.

Some Bible scholars believe that the offices of prominent scribes served as repositories for historical, literary, and prophetic texts. A room in the Temple complex would have been a secure place in which to store sacred texts—and a most appropriate one.

But these are merely guesses; and unless biblical archaeologists make some lucky discoveries, we may never know the truth.

· 2 ·

Greece and Rome

To the ancient Greeks the nine Muses—daughters of Zeus the all-father and Mnemosyne, goddess of memory—personified the arts and sciences. Epic poetry, lyric verse, love poetry, sacred hymns, choral dance and song, comedy, tragedy, history, astronomy each had its Muse. In their schools the Greeks built *mouseia*, temples to the Muses, and there they were served and worshiped.

The greatest of these was not in Greece itself, but on the northern coast of Egypt, where Alexander the Great had founded a new city. The Museion (Museum) of Alexandria was not only a center of scholarship; it served a political purpose as well. Alexandria was a Greek outpost in an ancient land whose royal cities and pyramids displayed the grandeur of its past. The museum helped to stamp Greek culture on Egyptian society.

The museum was part of the royal compound (the Brucheion), linked to the palace by a colonnade. Along this colonnade were three seating areas where scholars could discuss the books they read. The courtyards of the museum offered additional room for reading and discussion, and indoors a dining hall offered free meals to the resident scholars. Archaeologists believe that the library did not occupy a separate building, but was housed within the museum. Part of its building contained the library's administrative offices and workrooms for its staff, as well as the storerooms in which book-rolls were shelved. There may have been a reading room, but in the pleasant climate of Alexandria that would not have been a necessity.

The library collected the classic books of Greek poetry, and its scholars edited and arranged them and made them available for copying by the public. Alexandrian writers produced original prose and verse, commentaries on earlier works, and a considerable scientific literature. There were books by native historians on the countries that Alexander had conquered, and translations of the Hebrew scriptures and Egyptian chronologies.

The library obtained its books in many ways. It had substantial funds with which to buy from the bookshops of Athens and Rhodes, the centers of the Greek book trade. So eager were its librarians to complete their collections that they often fell victim to forgers, who found the counterfeiting of texts a profitable business. One ruler, Ptolemy III, ordered that all ships calling at the port be searched, and any books or manuscripts found aboard brought to the library. There copies were made and given to the owners, while the originals were added to the library's collections. This same monarch borrowed from the Athenians their official copies of the plays of the great tragedians Aeschylus, Sophocles, and Euripedes, depositing fifteen talents—equivalent to well over a million dollars in modern money—as security for their return. He kept the manuscripts, returned copies of them to Athens, and cheerfully forfeited his deposit.

Some of its books were produced by the library itself. The scholars of the museum wrote many volumes of prose and verse, and especially of commentaries on earlier works; these were deposited in the library. Translations were commissioned of important works in other languages.

The library staff faced a difficult task, for the books they received were in every state of completeness and preservation. They had no title-page, table of contents, or index, no chapter headings or running titles; sometimes not even the name of the author or the title of the book. Three-fourths of them were mixed rolls, containing more than one work; and larger books, such as the poems of Homer, would occupy several rolls. Unrolling a scroll in the hope that an incomplete volume might be identified from internal evidence was a time-consuming business.

The librarian was appointed by the king, and had to be courtier as well as scholar. He served as tutor to the children of the royal family, and selected books for the king's reading. Chosen from among the leaders of Alexandrian intellectual life, the librarians often advised the king on political as well as literary matters. This sometimes got them into trouble; but for the most part they devoted their energies to science and literature. Their library duties left them time to make substantial contributions to scholarship, and to serve the many scholars who came from other places to use the library.

❖   ❖   ❖

What became of this greatest of libraries?

Like many another institution of the Greek world, the library of Alexandria came to a lingering end. No single disaster destroyed its collections. A series of mishaps, combined with the attrition of centuries, put an end to the greatest library of the ancient world.

In 48 B.C.E., during Julius Caesar's brief Alexandrian War, a fire destroyed 400,000 rolls in the Royal Library. A smaller collection, housed in a temple called the Serapeum, remained intact. With its resources, and scrolls transferred from the Pergamene Library in Asia Minor, Alexandria still had books enough to meet the needs of scholarship.

After the Roman conquest of Egypt, the museum and library continued to exist, and scholarly work continued to be done in Alexandria. But Rome was now the center of intellectual life, and the leading thinkers and writers gravitated there.

Another more gradual conquest had its impact on Alexandria. With the triumph of Christianity, the human-centered pagan culture of ancient Greece gave way to the worldview of the church. Christians, so long persecuted by the state, now revenged themselves on their enemies, and fought each other over fine points of doctrine. By the time the Arab general 'Amr ibn-al-'As invaded Egypt in the 7th century, the people of Alexandria were ready to accept both the rule and the faith of their new masters.

'Amr, so the story goes, sought the advice of the Caliph Omar, leader of the faithful. What should be done with the books of the infidels? The answer came back from Medina: see if they agreed or disagreed with the teachings of the Koran. Books in accord with the Muslim holy book were unnecessary; those contradicting it were evil. The four thousand bath houses of Alexandria were heated for six months with the great library for fuel.

Is there any truth to this 11th-century legend? It was the Arabs who preserved the learning of the Greeks through the Dark Ages of the West. Would they wantonly destroy the literary treasures of Alexandria? Or should this crime against humanity be laid against Christian fanatics? Defenders of both religions have argued the point.

But by the time that 'Amr came to Alexandria, how much of the library remained? Neglect is as sure a destroyer of libraries as arson. How many of its rolls were eaten by mice or rotted by damp? How many were stolen, or removed by scholars to rescue them from danger?

Despite the best efforts of bishops and generals, fanatic mobs and invading armies, the glory of the Alexandrian Library did not vanish in any single disaster. Over the centuries it faded away.

◆　◆　◆

By the time that Rome changed from a republic into an empire in 31 B.C.E., it was the most powerful state in the Mediterranean world. But that was not enough; Rome wanted to be recognized as a civilized nation, heir to the Greek tradition. For two hundred years, Roman literature and Roman culture were modeled on Greek originals.

After Rome conquered Greece, ambitious Greeks found their way to Rome. Many served as tutors, for a knowledge of the Greek language and its literature soon became the hallmark of an educated Roman. Not only Greek teachers but also Greek books came in abundance to Rome, some through purchase and some as spoils of war.

The king of Pergamon, where a magnificent library had been built to rival that of Alexandria, sent the great scholar Crates of Mallos on a diplomatic mission to Rome. He was detained there by a broken leg; during his enforced stay he gave a series of lectures that created an interest in literary studies among the Romans. It is likely that he told his audiences of the Pergamene library and its treasures, for it can hardly be coincidental that the establishment of libraries in Rome began shortly after his visit.

The great Roman statesman Cicero maintained libraries at his palace on the Palatine Hill and his country estates, and made extensive use of them. He hired the Greek scholar Tyrannio to organize the library at his villa at Antium. "Since Tyrannio arranged my books," Cicero wrote to his friend Atticus, "the house seems to have acquired a soul."[6]

Not every Roman library was so heavily used. Fashionable Romans assembled libraries in their town houses and country homes. The architect Vitruvius gave detailed instructions on their construction. "Among cold baths and hot baths a library also is equipped as a necessary ornament of a great house," complained the philosopher Seneca, disparaging the man "who seeks to have book-cases of citrus-wood and ivory, who collects the works of unknown or discredited authors and sits yawning in the midst of so many thousand books, who gets most of his pleasure from the outsides of volumes and their titles." But Seneca urged his readers to "let just as many books be acquired as are enough, but none for mere show."[7]

The emperor Augustus boasted that he had found Rome a city of brick and left it a city of marble. He was determined to shape the city's form to reflect Rome's greatness—and his own. To this end he established two great public libraries, one in the Portico of Octavia in the Campus Martius, the other in the Temple of Apollo on the Palatine Hill near the imperial residence. Each contained a temple and separate chambers for Greek and Latin books. These two rooms were meant to proclaim Rome the equal of Greece in literary attainment. Later emperors followed Augustus's example, building libraries in Rome and Athens.

The great hall of an imperial public library served as reading

room and lecture hall. Some were brightened by artificial lighting, which not only helped readers on dark days but also
showed off the fine marble and expensive woods with which
they were decorated. In the storerooms the scrolls lay on open
shelves, with parchment labels hanging from wooden rollers.
Scientific works were produced in large format, while smaller
rolls were used for poetry. Books were brought to the reading
rooms for use there; they did not circulate except to the emper-
or and his closest friends.

Roman libraries were not limited to the capital; they were
found in provincial cities and resort towns across the empire.
Many were located within public baths, which served as social
and cultural centers. In the larger ones care was taken to keep
the scrolls well away from the steam baths, so that the highly
absorbent papyrus would not be damaged by moisture. Tivoli,
where wealthy Romans often summered, maintained a comprehensive Greek and Latin library, which even lent out books for
home reading.

◆   ◆   ◆

During Roman times the papyrus scroll remained the dominant medium for book publication. It would be several hundred years before it was replaced by the codex, the form of
book we know today. But that transition eventually did occur,
and there were several reasons for it. Animal skin is stronger
than papyrus, allowing longer works to be produced in one volume. Papyrus grew only in warm climates, while vellum (made
from calf skin) and parchment (made from sheep skin) could
be had wherever people ate meat. Their surface lent itself to
calligraphy and illustration, offering the possibility of the book
as a work whose physical beauty might equal—and even sur-
pass—its literary content. True, they were more difficult to pre-

pare than papyrus. But in the monasteries of Christian Europe there arose a class of men who had the time and the skill to devote to that task.

It was in fact the rise of the Christian church that stimulated the evolution of the book as we know it today. Just as animal skins replaced plant fibers, so the sewing of folded sheets between covers replaced the pasting together of flat sheets into rolls. The new medium made it possible to use both sides of the writing surface, and more sheets could be sewn between two covers than could be fastened to a roller. So it was possible to include all of Scripture within one volume; and it was easy to read that volume and find specific passages in it. There was another reason for Christians to embrace the codex: it served further to differentiate them from the Jews, for whom the Torah scroll was increasingly the emblem of their faith now that their Temple was destroyed.

By the beginning of the 4th century, the codex might be encountered as frequently as the roll. Two centuries later it had displaced the roll almost completely. Libraries converted their collections from papyrus rolls to vellum codices. This was a substantial project, and it required librarians to decide which books were worth the labor and expense of transcription. No doubt there were many writings that were not judged worthy, and were lost to us forever.

· 3 ·

Medieval Europe

I n four hundred years Christianity had become the dominant religion of the Roman Empire. As the organization of the Church began to imitate the pomp of empire, the simplicity of the monastic life attracted an increasing number of Christian men and women. Monte Cassino, "the mother cloister of all western monasticism,"[8] was founded in 529 by Benedict of Nursia, who established its system of government. This Benedictine Rule spread throughout Catholic Europe, and eventually came to govern almost every medieval monastery.

Western Europe was familiar with the Irish monks "who, for the mortification of their bodies, and salvation of their souls, live in exile from their country, and go about visiting holy places."[9] The Irish abbeys trained many monks who traveled to Britain or the Continent, establishing new monasteries from which to spread the faith. These foundations included scriptoria, where books were made, and libraries, where they were preserved.

One of the first of the Irish missionaries was Columba, often known as Columcille, who was born in 521 to one of Ireland's ruling families. As a student he would wander the country in search of books new to him. These he would copy, when he could get their owners' permission. In one famous instance he could not get permission, but copied the text anyway.

Columba's former teacher Finnian owned one of the finest book collections in Ireland. One of his treasures was Jerome's Latin translation of the Bible, which though completed over a century before was little known among the Irish. Finnian was so possessive of this book that Columba knew better than to ask permission to copy it. So he did it in secret, transcribing the manuscript by night. When Finnian discovered this, he demanded that Columba turn over the copy. The latter refused, and the matter was brought before Diarmit, the High King of Ireland. "Finnian's book has not decreased in value because of the transcript I made from it," Columba claimed. But Diarmit rendered a judgement based in the traditional Brehon law of Ireland: "To every cow her calf, to every book its transcript."[10] And he awarded the copy to Finnian.

This was the first copyright dispute in Western history; and it was one of the factors leading to Columba's exile from Ireland. Sailing across the Irish Sea, he founded on the island of Iona off the Scottish coast a monastery from which Christian teaching and Christian learning spread across northern Britain. At Iona the missionary monks studied and copied the Scriptures and the lives of saints, and trained generations of church leaders and scholars.

◆   ◆   ◆

The life of a monastic scholar was not an easy one. Thirteen hundred years ago in northern England, the prolific writer Bede complained that in addition to "innumerable duties in the monastery, I have to make my own shorthand notes while reading my sources, to copy out the passages I take from these, and to write my books themselves with my own hand."[11] But it was all for the glory of God and the salvation of men's souls, and Bede delighted in it.

One of Bede's students founded the cathedral school of York to train northern England's secular clergy, the priests who administered the sacraments and taught the rudiments of the Christian faith to their countrymen. The archbishop's devotion to learning and the efforts of its master Alcuin made the school's library the finest in Europe.

Traveling homeward in 782 from a mission to Rome, Alcuin met the Frankish ruler Charles the Great (Charlemagne). Impressed with his devotion to learning, Alcuin accepted the king's invitation to join his court and help with his ambitious plans to spread the Christian faith throughout his dominions. In his palace at Aachen, Charlemagne established a substantial library. This supplied the books that were read aloud each day to accompany his dinner: Charles was fond of history and of Augustine's *City of God*. The court library also included ancient Frankish poetry and texts on Germanic grammar, for Charlemagne was proud of his Frankish forebears. Ancient works were collected from across western Europe—"Who could even count the books which Your Majesty's decrees have gathered from every land?"[12] exclaimed a monk on Charlemagne's staff—and copies made from them spread classic texts to cathedrals and monasteries across Charlemagne's empire. Books on practical topics—architecture, surveying, agriculture, medicine, the art of war—helped to train the bureaucracy that ran the empire. Charlemagne expanded the Palace School, which had previously existed to tutor royal children, into a training college for leaders of church and state, and placed Alcuin at its head.

Under Charlemagne's direction and Alcuin's administration, monasteries played an increasing role in the multiplication of books and the teaching of letters. Charlemagne urged bishops and abbots throughout his realm "not to neglect the study of letters, but to learn eagerly for this end, that more easily and rightly you may penetrate the mysteries of the Divine Scriptures."[13] Teachers of grammar and music were to be appointed, so that in speech, writing, and chant the message of the Church might be made as attractive as possible to all. Acting on imperial orders, the monasteries translated the essential works of the Christian faith (the Lord's Prayer, the Creed, and the Benedictine Rule) into German, so that neither monk nor layman would be ignorant of its basic principles. Charlemagne's concern for the spread of knowledge extended to the smallest details: he even ordered that monasteries be provided with forests, where game might be hunted to furnish leather for bookbinding.

The Carolingian monastery was the hub of a self-contained community. It planted and harvested cereals and vegetables, baked bread and brewed beer, maintained fish ponds, herb gardens, and orchards, and tended flocks of poultry and herds of livestock. While monks were permitted meat only in case of serious illness, milk, cheese, and eggs were important parts of the monastic diet. The calves and lambs that they raised supplied vellum and parchment for monastic scribes, who wrote with quills supplied by the monastery's geese.

The library and scriptorium were vital parts of the monastery. On the northern side of the monastery church, a two-story building housed the scriptorium on the ground floor and the library on the upper level. This location provided both scribe and reader with diffused north light and protected them from the glare of the sun. The scriptorium provided books for the monastery's own use as well as for other monasteries and ecclestiastical and political leaders. Books to be copied were borrowed from other monasteries. Sometimes a scribe would be sent to a distant monastery to copy a book needed at his own cloister. Or a trade might be arranged, with two monasteries each copying a manuscript from its own library to fill a void in the other's collection. To speed up the process a borrowed book might be taken apart, allowing several copyists to work simultaneously. Manuscript copying was difficult work. The scribe Eadbeorht, a British monk at St. Gall, complained that "those who do not know how to write do not think that it is labor; it is true that only three fingers write, but the whole body toils."[14]

• • •

Why would a monastery need a library?

The Rule of St. Benedict made the reading of Christian literature a basic part of the monastic life. "Idleness is the enemy of the soul," declared the Rule. "Therefore, the brothers should have specified periods for manual labor as well as for prayerful reading." One of these reading periods was Sunday, when "all are to be engaged in reading except those who have been assigned various duties." As the Rule forbade private property of any sort, the brothers had to draw their books from a common store. The Rule's provisions for Lenten reading make this clear: "each one is to receive a book from the library, and is to read the whole of it straight through."[15]

Once a year, at a meeting of all the monks, the librarian read out the titles of the library's books and the names of the monks to whom they had been lent in the preceding year. As each brother deposited his book on the rug, the abbot asked him whether he had diligently studied his assignment. If he had, the brother was asked which book would be of use to him in the coming year and was given the desired book. But if the abbot thought the monk's choice unwise, he selected a more suitable one. If the brother had neglected his studies, he was not given a new book, but asked to read the old one for another year. In addition to the required individual reading, the monks listened to books while they dined. Saints' lives were often chosen for this purpose, and were read out in the refectory by brothers chosen for their strong voices and careful diction.

The library also served the monastery's teachers and administrators. Students learned the rudiments of grammar and composition by listening to their teachers read from the works of acknowledged masters, or from compilations of specimens illustrating various types of prose composition. More advanced instruction used the Roman orators Cicero and Quintilian as models of rhetoric, and Vergil and various Christian poets as textbooks of verse. Theology was taught from the Bible itself with the commentaries of the Church Fathers, and Pope Gregory I's *Book of Pastoral Care*. Other subjects included arithmetic and geometry, natural history, astronomy, and music.

The abbot and his deputies would need to consult law books and treatises on agriculture, surveying, and other aspects of estate management, for the monasteries often owned extensive farmlands. Composers of hymns and liturgical works prepared themselves by studying Christian and pagan poetry and works on grammar and poetics. The needs of the infirmary were served by medical anthologies, excerpting the works of the Greek physicians Galen and Hippocrates, and books on drugs and herbs.

Many of the books contained fine calligraphy and beautiful decorations. Parchment provided an excellent surface for rubrication—the use of red ink to highlight important words— and illumination—the use of miniature paintings to illustrate or decorate the text. Some books were covered in carved ivory tablets, others in leather-covered boards, still others in vellum wrappers.

Books were often lent to outside readers: bishops, secular clergy, the local nobility. Wealthy laymen and women borrowed books for Lenten reading; they were usually required to leave their own books, or other objects of equal value, as security against the borrowed books' return. When a book was lent, a notation would be made in the library catalog; another would be made to mark its return. Lending was done as a favor to the borrower, or as a courtesy to a powerful neighbor. There was no recognized right to borrow books, no public libraries that either an ancient Roman or a twentieth-century Westerner would recognize.

Monarchs, ecclesiastics, aristocrats, and scholars often owned small libraries. Books represented not only religion and scholarship but also wealth. The materials that went into a book were expensive—a 9th-century copy of the works of Vergil required more than fifty skins—and each volume represented a substantial expenditure of labor. Among the aristocracy, ownership of books, like possession of land, was a mark of wealth and social status. It had its practical side, too: law books and treatises on agriculture and military science covered topics of immediate interest to the nobility. Because books were so valuable—and so portable—a monastery would take the same precautions to protect its library as it would to safeguard its altar plate and priestly vestments. Among these precautions would be an inventory of its holdings; these evolved into library catalogs.

Despite these protective measures, the monasteries were often robbed of their books and other treasures. After Charlemagne's death, his empire became vulnerable to barbarian invaders. Many Irish monks were driven from their island by the Northmen, whose dragon ships brought robbery and destruction to any monastery within range of a seacoast or navigable river. The Saracens burst out of Arabia to conquer the Iberian peninsula, and destroyed many abbeys along the Mediterranean coast. And at St. Gall on the empire's eastern borders, the threat of Hungarian invasion forced the monastery to move its library to the more secure island stronghold of Reichenau.

◆ ◆ ◆

The universities of Europe arose to fill the void left when the Benedictine monasteries began to confine their educational activities to their own members. At first this task was inherited by the cathedral schools. Some of these had existed since Roman days, and others had been founded at the instigation of Charlemagne, to train church officials and priests. Many more came into existence in the newly emerging cities of a Europe that had rediscovered urban life. Both the reviving commercial life and the expansion of central governments required lawyers and administrators. The work of these men required an education beyond that provided monks or parish priests.

As students and teachers gathered—whether in major cities or isolated provincial towns—they organized to regulate their activities and secure recognition of their rights and privileges. The resulting corporate bodies were called "universities," from the Latin legal term for collective entities. The first of these arose in Bologna and Paris during the 12th century. Bologna's specialty was law, while Paris was renowned for theology. The University of Paris soon dominated the intellectual life of Christendom, and attracted students from all over Europe. It did not take long for monarchs and bishops to see the advantages of keeping their talented youth at home, and during the

13th and 14th centuries universities spread across western Europe.

The university undergraduate began his studies with the seven liberal arts. The *trivium* of grammar, rhetoric, and logic provided training in reasoning and argumentation: how can the truth be known, and how can it be conveyed to others? The *quadrivium* of arithmetic, geometry, music, and astronomy explained the natural laws governing the universe. The instructors were masters in the faculty of arts, who read the works of prescribed writers aloud to their students and amplified the text with their comments. Both students and faculty participated in debates that attempted to resolve difficult points.

The more ambitious young men remained at the university to study for higher degrees. The masters who lectured to the arts students were often themselves students in the higher faculty of theology. In many universities, faculties of medicine, civil law, and canon law prepared arts graduates for professional careers. In these higher faculties, as in the arts faculty, instruction consisted of masters reading to their students from prescribed texts and commenting upon them.

University teaching required books not only for reading aloud to students but also for preparation of disputations. At these public performances, a lecturer would state a question and then present both negative and positive answers to it, supporting both with extensive quotations from the Bible and the Church Fathers. These sources were consulted in the university libraries.

•   •   •

Unlike the Benedictine monks, whose Rule required them to borrow and read a single volume each year, advanced students in the universities often needed access to many books at once. A newly founded library would have only a small collection of books, housed in a locked chest or cupboard. The same room might contain a few desks for readers. As book collections grew larger, rooms were designed especially for their accommodation. The principal considerations were the maximization of natural light and the safe housing of large numbers of books. But even the largest of these collections was pitifully small by modern standards. In 1290, the richest library in Christian Europe, that of the Sorbonne in Paris, contained slightly more than one thousand books.

The typical scholarly library of the later Middle Ages was housed in an oblong room, three or four times longer than its width, with high vaulted ceilings. Its location on the upper floor of the monastery or college offered protection against floods and damp and burglars. Walls, floor, and ceiling were of stone or masonry as a protection from fire. The walls were usually painted green, to rest scholars' eyes. Large, high windows provided sunlight for the reader. There was no artificial light, and very seldom any heat in the library.

The large folio volumes, written in a clear hand, were kept on sloping surfaces on which a reader could rest the book he was using. These lecterns occupied the spaces between the windows, and were arranged perpendicular to the side walls of the library, on either side of a wide central aisle. The reader stood (or sat, if benches were provided) at the place where his book was chained.

To protect the books from theft, each was chained to a rod running alongside the desk top. Only by means of a key could a book be added to or removed from the collection. The administrator who kept the key was often made personally responsible for the safety of the collection.

Chaining was not the only evidence of the considerable care taken by medieval libraries to protect their books. The rules of the Sorbonne forbade the carrying of a light into the room, for fear of fire. Deliberate abuse of the books posed another danger to the collection.

Books were valuable property, often considered by their owners as too valuable to lend. Even though it was customary to pledge another book or item of equal value against its return, many monasteries threatened to excommunicate anyone who lent a book. At the Sorbonne, books would be lent to nonmembers only upon payment of a deposit sufficiently large to guarantee their return.

Another precaution against book theft relied upon spiritual rather than mechanical safeguards. Curses threatening excommunication, or worse, to anyone stealing or mutilating books were posted. One French abbey's catalog condemned book thieves to be "delivered to the fire of hell, [and] tormented endlessly."[17]

◆ ◆ ◆

The books themselves differed from those of the earlier monastic collections. The universities needed mass-produced texts, made as cheaply as possible. Thinner parchment, smaller pages, cramped writing, frequent use of abbreviations, more modest (and more portable) bindings—all were employed in the interest of practicality. The availability of paper, which was much cheaper than parchment, made the production of cheap books and multiple copies possible. While these were produced for the personal use of students and scholars, many found their way into university library collections.

It was during this period that many of the features we now expect to find in books came into being. The student or master in a hurry was well served by the tables of contents and subject indexes that began to appear in their books. Texts were subdivided, and chapters and verses established for the Bible. The underlining of quotations in red made the appeal to authority easier to sustain. These reference tools were especially useful to preachers composing their sermons. But many a reader had to rely on his memory rather than on any finding aids supplied with the book to find a once-read passage again.

University libraries were not limited to religious books. Although classical literature was not part of the university curriculum, the Latin writers (especially Vergil, Ovid, Horace, and the Roman historians) were read by scholars and collected by university libraries. Scientific collections were spotty, at best. Most common were elementary books on arithmetic and *computus* (the all-important art of calculating the dates of Easter and other movable feasts). Medical literature consisted of Hippocrates and Galen, as well as Muslim and Jewish books translated from Arabic into Latin. These formed the course of study in the university faculties of medicine. Universities where law was studied would have the Justinian Code and Gratian's *Decretum* as well as some of the extensive literature of legal commentary.

Almost all the books in a medieval library were in Latin, though there might be some devotional works, romances, or chronicles in the local language or that of a neighboring country. Rarely, a Greek or Hebrew psalter might be found, furnishing the only example of Scripture in its original languages.

·4·

China and India

The libraries of medieval Europe served the glory of God, but those of China were tools of the state. Though the Chinese have used writing for more than three thousand years, it was during the Chou dynasty (1122 to 256 B.C.E.) that Chinese literature truly began. A group of books produced during this period came to be known as the Five Classics. Later generations often called them the Confucian Classics, identifying them with the great moral philosopher K'ung fu-tzu, known to westerners as Confucius. His precepts for harmony and righteousness within the family and the state have shaped Chinese culture for twenty-five hundred years. They are set forth in a collection called the *Analects*, which quotes frequently from the Classics.

China gets its name from the Ch'in dynasty, which unified the country. Because this unification was opposed by Confucian scholars, Grand Councilor Li Ssu suggested to the emperor that all ancient books be burned. People who talked to each other about forbidden books, or who used their teachings to criticize the government, should be put to death. Those who did not not destroy their books were to be sent to build the Great Wall. The only books to be preserved were practical ones: those on medicine and pharmacy, agriculture and ways of predicting the future. Government officials, not the authors of ancient books, should tell the people what to think and do. This "burning of the books" did not succeed. Books were hidden by their owners, often in the walls of their houses; enough were preserved to assure the survival of the Confucian Classics.

The Ch'in empire lasted only fourteen years, from 221 to 207 B.C.E. It was succeeded by the Han (206 B.C.E. to 220 C.E.), whose imprint on the cultural life of China has lasted to our own century. The emperor convened great meetings at which scholars determined the correct interpretation of the Five Classics, and professors were maintained at court to expound them. The Han founded an imperial training school to educate candidates for high office; lower positions were filled by competitive examinations administered by the court scholars. An imperial library was formally established, to collect the officially approved versions of the Classics. Private possession of the Classics was once again permitted, and efforts were made to establish proper texts of these books and circulate them throughout the empire. Rewards were offered for the loan of books from private collections, and imperial agents scoured the country in search of texts, this time to preserve rather than to destroy them. As was the case in Alexandria, the generous bounty offered provided many with incentive for the forging of books.

Toward the end of the Han dynasty, the Five Classics and the *Analects* of Confucius were carved on stone steles on the grounds of the Imperial University. This was done in order to preserve the standard text that had so painstakingly been established. It took both sides of forty-six stones to contain the more than two hundred thousand characters. Scholars used them to make copies for study by stretching a thin sheet of moistened paper across the stone, brushing it into every character carved into the stele. After the paper was dry, ink was applied across it. This would leave blank the places where the paper had been pushed into the carved stone, producing a sheet of white writing on a black background. Government officials called "makers of rubbings" would provide copies upon payment of a fee.

The Han emperors were not motivated purely by a love of learning. Because they relied upon Confucian doctrine to justify their claim to rule China, they wanted to control the details of that doctrine. By using the Imperial Library to preserve the version of the Confucian Classics that supported their rule, and by making Confucian scholars dependent upon the government, they succeeded in harnessing the teachings of Confucius to their own purposes. Later rulers imitated this strategy, some going so far as to rewrite the Classics to serve the needs of the state.

◆   ◆   ◆

The first Chinese books were made of bamboo. Pages were prepared by cutting the hollow stem into cylinders, which were then split lengthwise into narrow tablets. The green skin that covered them was scraped off and the tablets dried over a fire. On each page a single vertical line of characters, each representing an entire word, was inscribed. There were several standard page sizes, ranging from eight inches to the twenty-eight-inch tablets used for the Classics, which held thirty characters each. The tablets were strung together with silk, hemp, or leather cords to make a book that could easily be rolled up for storage or travel.

Toward the end of the Han era, the Imperial Library copied bamboo books onto paper. Paper had been invented five centuries before, but was not used for writing for many years. It was a cheap writing material: a single worker could make two thousand sheets of paper in a single day. Compare the cost of one day's wages to the value of the two hundred animals whose skins were required to make one parchment or vellum codex in Europe.

As dynasties came and went, amid invasions and rebellions, both the Imperial Library and private collections suffered heavy losses. So important were books to the Chinese that every interval of peace saw attempts to re-create the collections that had been destroyed.

❖ ❖ ❖

For nearly four centuries after the fall of the Han dynasty, China was frequently divided into mutually hostile states. Even during this "Six Dynasties" period of disunity (220 to 589), the Imperial Library was maintained and cherished by China's rulers. When the country was reunified under the Sui (581 to 618) and the T'ang (618 to 907), scholars at the imperial court justified the new political order in Confucian terms. Thus the Sui and T'ang emperors, like their Han predecessors, had an interest in the text of the Confucian Classics and in the commentaries and dynastic histories that accompanied them on the shelves of Chinese libraries. Precedents were sought in earlier dynasties for T'ang policies. Creativity in finding appropriate precedent was a quality much valued in a court scholar.

"Though the empire had been won on horseback, it could not be governed on horseback."[18] As the imperial government became more complicated, the Imperial Library became more important. Its scholars provided the emperor with advice based on a sound knowledge of history and precedent, and produced and compiled documents for the state. This activity commanded more prestige than such worldly topics as law, medicine, and mathematics, subjects also studied in the imperial court.

The main task of the Imperial Library was to collect, preserve, and catalog the best of Chinese literature. Acceptance of a new work into the Imperial Library was the highest honor that could come to a new book. New commentaries on the Classics were added to established ones, providing that they did not stray from opinions approved by the government. The Bureau of Compositions, which was part of the Imperial Library, wrote prayers for the state rituals and supplied texts for official functions. These helped to sustain the emperor's claim that Heaven supported his right to rule the country. The History Office compiled dynastic histories, which served political as well as scholarly ends. By recounting the Chin dynasty's successful rule of a united China a thousand years earlier, they helped to demonstrate the legitimacy of T'ang rule.

Posts at the Imperial Library were greatly desired, and were awarded to some of the brightest young civil servants. These were selected by competitive examinations that tested knowledge of the Classics and talent in literary composition. This civil service examination system, with its emphasis on scholarship rather than high birth as a qualification for high office, stimulated the development of private libraries in families with ambitions for their sons.

A Chinese gentleman was expected to be an art lover and a scholar, or at least to behave like one. Many high officials, and some members of the imperial family, had a genuine love for literature and sought out the company of poets and scholars. Some achieved a reputation for literary accomplishment that has come down to our own time. Several of these amateur scholars accumulated substantial libraries and shared them with others. The Chin-dynasty collector Fan Wei not only opened his library but provided meals and lodging to the readers from across China who came to consult his books. Over one hundred scholars accepted his hospitality.

❖ ❖ ❖

As the T'ang dynasty came to an end at the beginning of the 10th century, the Imperial Library suffered serious losses. By the time the capital moved from Ch'ang-an to Lo-yang, its holdings had been reduced to ten thousand books. But under the Sung, who came to power in the latter half of the century, literature and scholarship revived.

The introduction of woodblock printing multiplied the copies of the Confucian Classics and other books, contributing to the growth of official libraries and private collections. As a skilled printer could produce well over a thousand copies in a day, the production of printed books was much cheaper than manuscript copies or stone rubbings. Thus it was possible to distribute a 130-volume edition of the Classics widely across China.

Sung government officials were encouraged to consult the library, where they might read such works as "The Comprehensive Mirror for Aid in Government," a detailed history whose title was chosen by the emperor himself. But only a few of the highest officials could borrow books. To discourage theft, Imperial Library books were copied onto special paper, making stolen copies readily identifiable and thus unsalable.

Even in more recent times the emperors took a serious interest in books and libraries. The 18th-century emperor Ch'ien-lung appointed a group of eminent scholars to compile a great anthology of Chinese literature: classics, history, philosophy, and literary collections. Books in the Imperial Library and other collections were examined, and selected works were transcribed into uniform volumes for this "Complete Library of the

Four Treasures." The project took nearly twenty years and employed fifteen thousand copyists. It produced seven hand-written copies, each containing more than thirty-six thousand volumes. Each set was housed in its own building. Copies have survived to our day in Beijing and Taipei.

This was not entirely a matter of literary preservation. The same process of searching libraries that identified and collected those books to be preserved also served to identify those writings that met with imperial disfavor. "None may remain to after generations," the emperor decreed, "in order to cleanse our speech and make straight the hearts of man."[19] Such works were destroyed, so thoroughly that hundreds of books known to have existed before Ch'ien-lung's time have perished completely. On one day it was reported that 52,840 woodblocks for printing "seditious works" had been broken up to use for firewood. As with the burning of the books two thousand years before, this "inquisition of Ch'ien-lung" demonstrated that the Chinese well knew the power of the written word.

◆　◆　◆

The written word was slower to make its mark on Indian life, whose dominant Brahman tradition was transmitted orally from generation to generation. Religious knowledge was the exclusive province of a small priestly caste, who had no interest in reducing it to writing. But two religions arose that did not share this reluctance to write down sacred texts. To both Jains and Buddhists the path to salvation lay through spiritual discipline rather than the performance of ritual. Jainism and Buddhism developed canons of scripture over the following centuries. Both maintained monasteries as religious and educational centers.

Some of the Buddhist monasteries attracted students from all over India. We are told that in the 5th century the Jetavana monastery had "chapels for preaching and halls for meditation, mess-rooms and chambers for the monks, bathhouses, a hospital, libraries and reading rooms with pleasant shady tank [pond] and a great wall encompassing all."[20] As Buddhism spread across Asia, devotees from other lands made pilgrimage to the Indian monasteries. The most famous was Nalanda, whose collection of Buddhist manuscripts attracted scholars and pilgrims from as far away as China.

Tibetan accounts tell us that it took three large buildings to contain Nalanda's library. One of them, the Ratnadadhi (Ocean of Gems), was nine stories high. The books were placed flat on wooden shelves divided into compartments, with the most valuable manuscripts stored in heavy wooden chests. Tradition holds that a huge inkpot provided the means for many students to copy books simultaneously from dictation. The 7th-century Chinese pilgrim Hsuan-Tsang copied many manuscripts at Nalanda and brought them back to his native China. When he returned to Ch'ang-an he deposited his treasures in the Hung-fu monastery, and spent the rest of his life translating the books he had brought back from India.

Whether all these books were brought back in Chinese or in Indian form is uncertain. Indian books certainly differed in form from Chinese scrolls. They were usually written on palm leaves: young leaf buds cut open, boiled for several hours, dried in the sun for several days, cooled by moonlight, and smoothed and trimmed. This offered a writing surface of perhaps four by twelve inches, allowing ten lines of text—though this varied from book to book. The pages were pierced in the center and held together with string, then covered with wooden boards, which were often lacquered and brightly painted. Leather bindings were not used, as animal skin was not considered a suitable material for religious literature. Instead the books were wrapped in cloth.

The Buddhist love of books left behind a substantial monument that was discovered by Western explorers in 1907. Near Tun-Huang, in the desert of Chinese Turkestan, lie the Caves of the Thousand Buddhas. In one of these caves a chamber was sealed up almost a thousand years ago, probably to protect its contents from Mongol raiders. The dry Turkestan climate has preserved over fifteen thousand paper rolls, some dated sixteen hundred years ago. Most are in Chinese, but among them are texts in Tibetan, Sanskrit, Iranian, Turkic—and even a Hebrew-language anthology of selections from the Bible. Did the Tun-Huang hoard constitute a monastic library, or was it merely a scrap heap of manuscripts discarded by the neighboring monasteries when they were replaced by printed copies? There is no agreement among the scholars who have studied them.

1. Cuneiform Clay Tablet of the *Epic of Gilgamesh*—This relic from King Assurbanipal's library in ancient Nineveh is now in the British Museum. (Department of Western Asiatic Antiquities, no. K 3375)

2. The Library of Alexandria in Ptolemaic Times—In this drawing by Roy G. Krenkel, Hellenic scholars are shown examining scrolls and discussing their contents. By comparing manuscripts and assessing their authority, the scholars of Alexandria put together definitive texts of Homer and the other great writers of ancient Greece. (Used by permission of Barry Klugerman, literary executor for the Krenkel estate.)

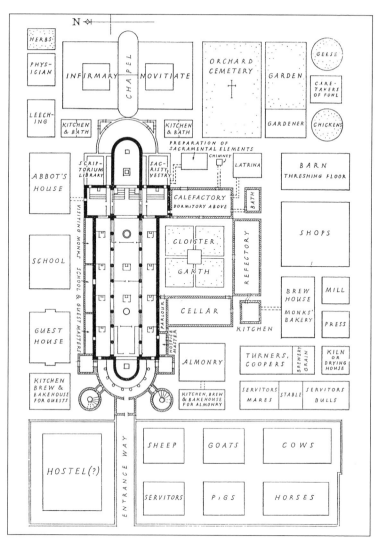

N ⟶

HERBS

PHYS-ICIAN

INFIRMARY

CHAPEL

NOVITIATE

ORCHARD CEMETERY

GARDEN

GEESE

CARE-TAKERS OF FOWL

LEECH-ING

KITCHEN & BATH

KITCHEN & BATH

GARDENER

CHICKENS

PREPARATION OF SACRAMENTAL ELEMENTS

CHIMNEY

ABBOT'S HOUSE

SCRIP-TORIUM LIBRARY

SAC-RISTY VESTRY

LATRINA

BARN THRESHING FLOOR

CALEFACTORY DORMITORY ABOVE

BATH

VISITING MONKS

CLOISTER

REFECTORY

SHOPS

SCHOOL

SCHOOL & GUEST MASTER

GARTH

BREW HOUSE

MILL

CELLAR

MONKS' BAKERY

PRESS

PARLOUR

KITCHEN

GUEST HOUSE

HOSPICE MASTER

ALMONRY

TURNERS, COOPERS

BREWING GRAIN

KILN OR DRYING HOUSE

KITCHEN BREW & BAKEHOUSE FOR GUESTS

KITCHEN, BREW & BAKEHOUSE FOR ALMONRY

SERVITORS MARES

STABLE

SERVITORS BULLS

ENTRANCE WAY

SHEEP

GOATS

COWS

HOSTEL (?)

SERVITORS

PIGS

HORSES

3. The Perfect Monastery—This English-language rendering of the Plan of St. Gall (circa 820) shows the ideal arrangement for a self-contained community devoted to the service of God. The monastery of St. Gall, in today's Switzerland, was built to an approximation of this plan. The library and scriptorium were located at the north end of the chapel, to secure the best light for reading and copying manuscripts. Cattle and sheep provided parchment and leather (for bookbinding), and geese furnished quills to make pens. (From Kenneth John Conant, *Carolingian and Romanesque Architecture, 800-1200*, Penguin, 1966; used by permission of the Yale University Press.)

4. Medieval Scribes at Work—This illumination from the 11th-century Gospel Book of Emperor Henry III shows two monks writing in the scriptorium of the abbey of Echternach (now in Luxembourg). Perhaps a third monk is dictating to them, for each has only one book open in front of him. (Universitätsbibliothek Bremen, Ms. b. 21, f. 124v.; Copyright Dr. Ludwig Reichert Verlag, Wiesbaden)

5. Albertus Magnus Lecturing to Students at the Sorbonne—One of the great Dominican scholars, Albert taught at Paris from 1245 to 1248. In this illumination from *Le Livre des propriétés des Choses* he is reading from a text to students who are taking notes on his commentary. The age of his listeners suggests that they are theology students. (Reims, B.M., Ms. 993, fol. 200; Courtesy of Bibliothèque Municipale, Reims, France)

6. The Big Wild Goose Pagoda, Ch'ang-an (present-day Xi'an), China—It was here that Hsuan-Tsang deposited the Buddhist manuscripts that he brought back from his pilgrimage to India. Though often restored over the intervening centuries, this is substantially the same building that the Emperor Kao-tsung built. (Photograph by Dr. Glen Dudbridge, in Sally Hovey Wriggins, *Xuanzang: A Buddhist Pilgrim on the Silk Road*, Westview Press, 1996)

7. House of Wisdom, Baghdad—In this drawing by Trevor Newton, a scholar consults a book, perhaps in preparation for a disputation before the library's founder, the 'Abbasid caliph al-Mamun. (From *Aramco World*, March-April 1987, by permission of the publishers)

8. Manuscript from the Urbino Library—This page from an illuminated manuscript of the Bible illustrates both Duke Federigo's exquisite taste and the sublime craftsmanship of the Florentine artisans who produced it. Little wonder that the popes coveted Federigo's books—and brought them to the Vatican Library, where they remain today. (Ms. Urbinate Lat. 1, f.27.r., Bibliotèca Apostolica Vaticana, Rome)

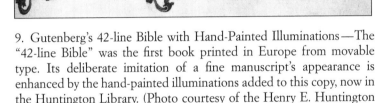

9. Gutenberg's 42-line Bible with Hand-Painted Illuminations—The "42-line Bible" was the first book printed in Europe from movable type. Its deliberate imitation of a fine manuscript's appearance is enhanced by the hand-painted illuminations added to this copy, now in the Huntington Library. (Photo courtesy of the Henry E. Huntington Library and Art Gallery, San Marino, California)

10. Bibliotheca Laurentiana, Florence—Designed by Michelangelo, this library was built to house the book collections built up by the Medicis. The books were chained to metal rods to prevent their removal. Stored flat on shelves below the sloping lecterns, books could be raised to eye level for convenience in reading. The card at the end of each lectern lists the books housed there. (Photo by Alinari)

11. Göttingen University Library in the 19th Century—This engraving by I. Poppel (after a drawing by O. Eberlein) shows Europe's greatest academic library in the era when it made such a strong impression on visiting American scholar George Ticknor, later one of the founders of the Boston Public Library.

· 5 ·

The Islamic World

When the Arabs, inspired by the teachings of the prophet Muhammad, swept forth out of the desert in the 7th century, they had no literature save the Koran. Within three hundred years, Muslim libraries spread from Spain to India, across lands that had been parts of the Roman, Byzantine, and Persian empires. The Arabs held a great respect for the civilizations that they conquered, and found in the learning of the Greeks, the Persians, and the Jews a source of awe and inspiration. Though the poet Al-Mutannabi proclaimed that "the most honourable seat in this world is in the saddle of a horse," he added that "the best companion will always be a book."[21]

Like Judaism and Christianity, Islam was a religion based on books. The Koran contained the word of God, as revealed to the prophet Muhammad. To interpret its teachings, the sayings of Muhammad's companions (the *hadith*) were collected and studied. Variant readings of the Koran, and explanations of its more complex passages, were produced by a multitude of commentators. Legal opinions, sermons, and accounts of disputations recorded the lively jurisprudence of Islam.

Literary studies were also important to Muslims. Grammar and etymology aided in the understanding of the Koran. Genealogy and history were needed to establish the succession of political and religious authority. And the study of geography and languages were essential to the administration of the ever-widening Islamic realm. Influenced by the ancient literary traditions of Byzantium and Persia, the Arabs studied the philosophical sciences: medicine, astronomy, geometry, philosophy. It was through their work that Christian Europe received the inspiration for the Renaissance.

The earliest Arab books were written on papyrus, parchment, or poplar bark; like those of their Christian neighbors, the sheets were gathered and bound into codices, rather than pasted together into scrolls. In 751 the art of papermaking was introduced from China into Samarkand, from which it soon spread across the Islamic world. The resulting abundance of paper lowered the price of books throughout Islam, and the bookshops that arose in every Arab city fostered a lively literary culture. With its emphasis on the importance of reading the Koran, and the reverence for learning in general that the veneration of the Koran inspired, Islamic culture ensured a high degree of literacy.

•   •   •

Two centuries after Muhammad, the caliph al-Mamun founded the Bayt al-hikma ("house of wisdom") in his capital city, Baghdad. Modeled after the Museum of Alexandria, it was a center of scholarly activity. There books were translated from Greek, Syriac, and Persian, and new works were commissioned from Arab historians and scientists.

Members of the staff lived in the Bayt al-hikma, where they were on call day and night to serve the caliph's needs. A group of Islamic scholars was maintained to conduct disputations before the caliph. But its library was the most important of its activities. Known throughout the Muslim world, it attracted readers from many countries. Even scholars making the sacred pilgrimage to Mecca found the Bayt al-hikma too attractive to leave.

Many individual scholars had their own libraries, and the funds with which to maintain them. They collected rare and curious books in such fields as philosophy, logic, geometry, arithmetic, music, medicine, and astrology, and paid translators well for rendering sought-after works into Arabic. Though they were privately owned, many of these libraries were made available for the use of the learned community. Scholars, translators, commentators, compilers, and writers used them, as did courtiers who might well have found it useful to read up on the caliph's favorite topics of learned conversation.

In less than a hundred years, true public libraries began to appear. These institutions were called *dar al-'ilm* (hall of science). The first was founded by Ibn Hamdan in Mosul, at the very beginning of the 10th century. Its collection included books on all subjects, with an emphasis on philosophy and astrology, two fields especially dear to its founder. All were welcome there. Lectures were given on the premises. Foreign scholars were provided not only with ink and paper but also with food and drink.

A similar institution was founded in 996 by Sabur ibn Ardasir in Baghdad. Housed in a building of marble and limestone, it contained 10,400 volumes. Even though religious books dominated, the library included grammar and philology, medicine and philosophy, astronomy and geology. Sabur's *dar al-'ilm* was one of Baghdad's primary cultural centers, frequented by scholars, poets, and musicians. Many scholars donated books and money to Sabur's *dar al-'ilm*, but only definitive texts of significant works were allowed onto its shelves.

When the Muslims invaded Spain in the 8th century, they brought their love of learning with them. Their capital, Córdoba, was the most cultured city in Europe. Its book bazaar and its many libraries attracted scholars from all over the Islamic world as well as travelers from the countries of Christian Europe. In the university of Córdoba, the greatest center of learning of Islam, mathematics, astronomy, and medicine were studied. At its peak the royal library had five hundred people on its payroll, including copyists, illuminators, and bookbinders. Its agents bought and copied scholarly manuscripts in Alexandria, Baghdad, and Damascus. It took forty-four substantial books just to list the four hundred thousand volumes in its collection.

In Cairo the Dar al-hikma (hall of wisdom) was open to all: "Whoever wanted was at liberty to copy any book he wished to copy, or whoever required to read a certain book found in the library could do so."[22] Its superb library covered every category of science and letters, with books written out by the finest calligraphers of Egypt. The caliph provided not only salaries for librarians and caretakers, but also paper, pens, and ink for library users.

Whether from a love of learning or from a conviction that a great library was a sign of a glorious empire, succeeding caliphs continued to found and maintain libraries. Before the Mongol invasion of the mid-13th century there were thirty-six collections in Baghdad that were open to scholars, of which at least twenty were genuine public libraries.

❖   ❖   ❖

The Arab book collector was typically a member of the royal family or a high government official. Unless he had a scholarly interest in a particular field, his library would include all areas of knowledge, emphasizing languages, literature, and history. The value of a book lay not in its rarity or subject matter, but in the beauty of its calligraphy. The Arab bibliophile collected not only fine books but also fine copyists, men renowned for accuracy and beautiful work. Many copyists were employed by collectors, while others were independent craftsmen, producing books to order.

Bibliophiles insisted on complete and accurate texts, retaining noted scholars to collate and correct them. They especially treasured works in the handwriting of their original authors and often extended their patronage to living writers, who repaid their support by dedicating their works to their patrons. Some collectors would commission a major work from a writer and insure its uniqueness by not allowing anyone to copy it.

Scholars built their collections by copying and by purchase. As students, they copied scientific works from the dictation of their professors. In later life, they copied books in public libraries and in private collections made available to them. Even when they bought books—there was a flourishing book trade throughout the Islamic world—they would collate, correct, and annotate them. Given the cost and effort of acquiring books, most scholars limited their collecting to books in their specialties or containing knowledge needed in their work. Religious scholars collected only books conforming to the doctrines of their particular sect.

Collectors were careful to ensure that their books would be well used after their deaths. Passing sometimes through a chain of heirs, their collections would be deposited in public or institutional libraries, there to remind future generations of the taste and wisdom of those who had assembled them. Writers, too, donated their books to libraries, to ensure that their scholarship—and their reputations—would outlast their lives.

* * *

What did a great Islamic library look like?

Entering through an oblong portico, the visitor would pass through a second doorway leading into an ornately ornamented room. Its marble floor would be covered with straw mats in summer and with felt rugs and woolen cushions in winter. Curtains covered the windows and doors, offering both books and readers protection from the sun. In winter, they kept out the cold. Running water was piped into the building where a fountain provided for both washing and drinking. A separate room served as the copyists' workshop. Some scribes worked individually; others might work in groups, copying to dictation so as to produce several copies of the same book.

A smaller library would present a more modest appearance. Whether housed in a room of its own, or in a glass-fronted cabinet in a hallway, its location would be in the most prominent part of the building. Books were considered useful as well as ornamental; in colleges, classes would be held nearby so that the books could be referred to as needed.

In any case the books would be housed in wooden cabinets, often ornamented with calligraphic carvings. These cabinets contained several shelves, each divided vertically to form a series of pigeonholes, in which the books lay on their sides in stacks. The books were arranged in descending order from the sacred to the ordinary. Three divisions emerged: religious sciences (Koran, theology, and law), those sciences required to support religious studies (literature, philology, and history), and philosophical sciences (medicine, astronomy, and mathematics). A locked glass door simultaneously protected and displayed the books; but the protection it offered from theft and dust was offset by the encouragement such an environment offered to the growth of insects. Books were kept away from the floor to avoid damage from humidity.

A visitor entering the library might request a specific book of the librarian, or request that the library's catalog be brought to him. Paper and ink would be provided for him to make notes, but if he intended to copy the entire book he would have to furnish his own supplies and obtain the librarian's permission. Although this might be denied in a private collection, to maintain the rarity or indeed uniqueness of its holdings, it was almost always permitted in public libraries. Some poor scholars earned their living by visiting the great libraries and making copies for sale of their most important books.

The visitor would sit on the floor or on a cushion, his back leaning against a wall. The book would rest atop his crossed legs, or on a small wooden table in front of him. In the palm of his left hand he would hold the paper on which his right hand wrote with a reed pen. Readers were warned not to place books on the ground, nor to hold an ink-filled pen over a book from which one might be copying or making notes. When he was finished, the visitor would hand the book back to the librarian and request another, or leave the library.

Many libraries did lend books, considering it a religious obligation to facilitate copying and study. The 13th-century Spanish Arab historian Ibn Hayyan cited the generosity of libraries to explain why he never bought books: "Whatever book I want to have I can get on loan from any library, while if I wanted to borrow money to buy these books I should find no-one who would lend it to me."[23]

To prevent loss or damage to the books, they were lent only to readers who could be trusted to respect them and not to allow them to become lost, soiled, or damaged. When this could not be taken for granted, a prospective borrower might be obliged to leave a sum of money or an item of equal value to ensure the book's return. Typically the period of a loan was one day for each leaf of text; this was considered ample time for the borrower to copy the entire book. In some cases, rather than lend a book to a powerful official who might not choose to return it, its owner would have a copy made to give to the would-be borrower.

Most libraries were open to all Muslims, rich and poor alike. Although some endowment charters specified that only orthodox Muslims, or those adhering to a particular sect, were to be admitted, in practice even those restrictions were often ignored by administrators and librarians.

◆ ◆ ◆

What became of the great Islamic libraries?

Not every caliph was a scholar, and many rulers found better use for their funds than the maintenance of libraries. To some of them, libraries were storehouses from which to bestow gifts on their favorites; to others, mere collections of waste paper.

When Saladin conquered Egypt in 1175, he allowed his followers to help themselves to the treasures of Al-Hakim's Dar al-hikma. When the Umayyid dynasty ended in Spain and the caliphate was divided among smaller kings, the royal library was dispersed. In 1499, after the Christian conquest of Spain, eighty thousand Muslim books were burnt in Granada. Other Islamic libraries had been destroyed by the Crusaders as they swept through Syria and Palestine in the 12th century. But Christians were not the only ones whose bigotry drove them to despoil Islamic libraries. Many were destroyed by orthodox Muslims intent upon suppressing heretical books.

When the Mongols swept across the Muslim lands in the 13th century, they destroyed the great cities of central Asia and, in 1258, Baghdad itself. In one week most of that city's thirty-six public libraries were destroyed. Al-Nadim's *Fihrist al'ulum* (Index of the sciences) lists the books known to a 10th-century Baghdad scholar; fewer than one in a thousand survives today because of the Mongol raids. Illuminated manuscripts and exquisite examples of calligraphy were burned as fuel, while finely decorated leather bindings went to shoe Mongol feet. Scholars and students were massacred, and the Mongol hordes rode westward across Syria until they were stopped in Egypt.

Did the Mongols despise learning entirely? The year after he destroyed Baghdad, the Mongol leader Hulagu built an astronomical observatory at Maraghah, near Lake Urmiyah in Azerbaidjan. A neighboring library housed—if we may believe the chroniclers—four hundred thousand volumes, the spoils of conquest from Syria, Mesopotamia, and Persia. What use did he make of these riches? Here the chronicles are silent.

·6·

The Printed Book

After Johann Gutenberg issued the first mass-produced Bible in the early 1450s, the art of printing spread rapidly across Europe. By 1500, there were two hundred sixty places where it was practiced. Tens of thousands of titles had been published, and at least ten million volumes had come off the presses. Almost half of these were Bibles, prayer books, and other standard Christian texts. But more than half were literary, historic, or scientific books.

Printers in Venice and Basel issued scholarly editions of the Greek and Latin classics and the Church Fathers that were acclaimed throughout Europe. These books stimulated scholarship as much by their uniformity as by their authenticity: having the same words on the same page in every copy made it possible for scholars to compare and discuss texts. The printed book was much cheaper than the manuscript: an octavo volume cost an educated man only a day's pay or two. The printed octavo was portable as well as affordable, a boon to the diplomat or secretary who spent much of his time traveling— or waiting.

In the 15th century, church councils proceeded at a leisurely pace, often lasting for several years. Council business often required the borrowing of documents from monastic collections, while lengthy recesses in the proceedings afforded prelates and secretaries ample opportunity to visit nearby monasteries in search of literary manuscripts. They found many texts that had been lost since Roman times, and sent these to scholars to be edited and published.

Both Catholic and Protestant leaders saw in the printing press a valuable resource in the struggle for ideological supremacy within Christendom. Both sides viewed libraries as arsenals of intellectual weaponry. Without libraries, said the Dutch Jesuit Peter Canisius, "we are like soldiers who march into battle without any weapons."[24] A good library, said the Lutheran jurist and mathematician Gottfried Wilhelm Leibniz, "would contain material to defend the true religion against its adversaries."[25]

◆ ◆ ◆

It was in private collections that the greatest progress was made in the establishment and use of libraries. Under the influence of the humanist movement, which sought to revive the literary tradition of Greece and Rome, monarchs, nobles, and wealthy merchants began to build serious libraries.

In the Italian city of Florence, bookseller Niccolo de' Nicoli was so enthusiastic a collector that, though originally a wealthy man, he died heavily in debt. He made his books available to those who would read or copy them, and he lent them freely to his friends. Although he knew almost no Greek, he collected Greek books so that scholars might be able to consult them. After Niccolo's death his books went to his friend and patron Cosimo de' Medici, who directed the political life of Florence as well as an international business empire. Cosimo divided Niccolo's books between his private collection, housed in a splendid room in the Medici palace, and the public collection that he had established in the Franciscan monastery of San Marco in Florence.

The library housing this collection was a long, narrow, vaulted room, divided into three parts by rows of columns. The books were distributed among sixty-four lecterns fashioned from cypress wood. They were not crowded together: none of the lecterns held more than six volumes. As the collection grew in size, a "Greek library" was added. In this room were placed all the non-Latin books, Greek as well as the few in Arabic, Armenian, and Hebrew.

Cosimo's grandson Lorenzo "the Magnificent" surrounded himself with artists and scholars, and enlarged Cosimo's library to well over one thousand manuscripts. Almost half of these were in the Greek language. Lorenzo sent the scholar John Lascaris to Constantinople for Greek manuscripts, where he acquired several hundred. Many of them contained texts previously unavailable in Italy. Lorenzo also collected Italian literature. Florentine humanists borrowed liberally from his collection, often transcribing books so that they might have their own copies. Lorenzo's books, together with those Cosimo had placed in San Marco, were moved in 1571 to the Bibliotheca Laurentiana in Florence, a marble palace designed by Michelangelo. There they remain today.

Federigo da Montefeltro, Duke of Urbino, was a rival to the Medicis at book collecting. He put thirty or forty copyists to work, a contemporary biographer tells us, and sought the catalogs of other libraries in order to ensure that his collection surpassed theirs. In this library "all books were superlatively good, and written with the pen, and had there been one printed book it would have been ashamed in such company."[26] Vespasiano de Bisticci, a bookseller who helped Cosimo de' Medici, Duke

Federigo, and Pope Nicholas V to build their libraries, goes on to claim that this library contained the complete works of all known writers, ancient and modern, sacred and profane, whether composed in the classic languages or written in Italian. No doubt he exaggerates; but a contemporary inventory of the Urbino library lists 1,104 manuscripts, including many in Greek and Hebrew. Among Latin books, there were many examples of classical, patristic, and humanist texts, beautifully decorated by the miniaturists of Ferrara and Florence. Every book in his collection was written on vellum, bound in crimson, ornamented with silver.

The collection occupied a room twenty-two feet by forty-five. Clear north light came through windows set high in the twenty-three-foot walls, which were lined with bookshelves. Latin verses in praise of books and libraries were inscribed on the cornices. A large bronze eagle served as a lectern. In the small study adjacent, carved armchairs surrounded a reading table. But the Duke's books served him for recreation as well as study: he maintained at his court five men to read aloud during meals. Except during Lent, when spiritual works were read, the Duke listened to the Roman historian Livy—in Latin.

Federigo da Montefeltro's descendant, Duke Francis Mary II, bequeathed the collection to the citizens of Urbino to be maintained as a public library. But Pope Alexander VII, who claimed that he wished to ensure "their preservation and proper treatment,"[27] had the books taken to Rome. In 1658 they were incorporated into the Vatican Library, "for the increase of the splendor of the Holy See, and the benefit of Christendom."[28]

The Bibliotèca Vaticana, today one of the world's great treasure houses, traces its founding to 1450. Pope Nicholas V used money collected during that jubilee year—when one hundred thousand pilgrims, bearing contributions to Church coffers, flocked to Rome—to augment the surviving papal collection. He donated 340 manuscripts from his own collection, and purchased additional books with church funds. He sent agents across Europe in search of books, and bought manuscripts from the Imperial Library of Byzantium when Constantinople fell to the Turks. He employed Byzantine scholars to translate Greek manuscripts into Latin, and hired copyists from Florence and Bologna to produce new copies of Latin classics. At his death in 1455, the Vatican Library had grown to 1,209 volumes.

Nicholas's successors maintained the library and opened it to scholars outside the Vatican. Sixtus IV declared in 1475 that the library's purpose was "to serve the dignity of the serving church, to further the faith, [and] for the use and honor of scholars and all those who are devoted to the study of sciences."[29] He had a large suite of rooms in the Vatican Palace outfitted for the purpose, and employed some of the finest artists and craftsmen in Italy in their construction and decoration. Great artists and writers sought inspiration in the Vatican Library: the architect Donato Bramante, the writer Baldassare Castiglione, and the painter Raphael were among them.

•   •   •

Elsewhere in Europe, a generation of bibliophiles arose for whom the printed book was as worthy of a place in their collections as the manuscript.

A young medical student in Paris offered to provide wealthy aristocrats with "instructions concerning erecting of a library." Gabriel Naudé urged the beginning bibliophile to seek the advice of more experienced collectors and to obtain copies of every available library catalog, ancient or modern. And he should collect as many books as possible: every book, no matter how bad, will someday be wanted by somebody. "For certainly there is nothing which renders a Library more recommendable, than when every man findes in it that which he is in search of, and could no where else encounter."[30]

Naudé urged collectors to open their libraries to the public. There is no point in collecting books, he asserted, unless they are made available to any who can make use of their contents. Books should be lent for limited periods of time to "persons of merit and knowledge"; but careful records should be kept. A good librarian should be hired to make this possible, and to produce two catalogs: one by subject, and one by author. The latter would help to identify books needed to complete the collection, and prevent purchasing the same book twice. It would also assist those who wished to read all the works of a particular writer.

•   •   •

In 1524, Martin Luther urged the councilors of all the cities in Germany to "erect and conduct Christian schools." These were to educate Protestant Germany's political, commercial, and religious leaders; and they would need libraries to gather together and make available the books needed to guide a Christian community. "No effort or expense should be spared to provide good libraries or book repositories, especially in the larger cities which can well afford it,"[31] Luther proclaimed, citing Paul's epistles in support of the importance of reading. He blamed the sorry state of German education on the fact that "men failed to found libraries but let the good books perish and kept the poor ones."[32] He would stock libraries with the Holy Scriptures and the best commentaries on them; books useful for learning the languages of the Bible; chronicles and histories; and books on law and medicine. Other Protestant reformers offered similar advice, claiming that libraries would encourage young people to improve their souls during time they might otherwise spend in taverns or bowling greens.

Despite the enthusiasm with which German cities established public libraries, Luther's dream was only partially realized, doomed by the lack of resources on the part of city governments and lack of interest among the clergy. The libraries became treasuries in which rare books and manuscripts were preserved. Except for historical and legal documents, the public libraries had little to offer. Used mostly by teachers and pastors, their contents reached the general public only indirectly, as reflected in classroom lectures and Sunday sermons.

◆ ◆ ◆

The printing press had at first only a limited impact on university libraries. Despite the great discoveries being made by scientists and explorers and communicated in print to the learned world, neither the university curriculum nor the composition of the student body changed to any great extent. The role of the university was to defend orthodoxy in religion and philosophy, and to educate administrators for the needs of church and state, not to contribute new learning to the store of human knowledge.

More often than not the library was ornamental rather than useful: a storehouse for valuable gifts, a repository of learned manuscripts, but not at all an essential part of the students' educational experience. University libraries were rarely accessible to students. Typically they were open only a few hours a week. Such lending as they did was to professors only.

Their fortunes ebbed and flowed with the tides of war and politics. Some were burned or plundered by invading armies or appropriated by powerful nobles. In 1550, during the English Reformation, royal commissioners visited Oxford. They removed painted windows, religious ornaments, and other "popish" elements from the university, and pillaged its libraries. Books were taken from the shelves "some to serve their jakes [latrines], some to scour their candlesticks, and some to rub their boots."[33]

The library that Duke Humfrey, youngest brother of King Henry V, had provided in the middle of the 15th century was totally destroyed. It was not restored until 1598, when Thomas Bodley undertook to reestablish a "public library" for the university. By Bodley's death fifteen years later his library contained fifteen thousand works in seven thousand volumes. Almost all the books were in Latin. English was not considered a scholarly language, and Bodley thought English literature too frivolous and transitory for a university library. But Bodley was ahead of his time in his enthusiasm for oriental languages. He arranged for the acquisition of books in Greek, Hebrew, Arabic, Turkish, and Persian, and even added titles in Chinese, though there was nobody in Oxford who could read them.

·7·

Kings and Congressmen

For as long as the book has been in existence, there have been book lovers and book collectors. In the age of the manuscript book, only the wealthy could afford private book collections. Even when the spread of printing made books affordable to a wide range of people, there were still many collectors who loved to display the splendor and wealth embodied in a fine library.

Popes and princes were institutions as well as people, and their book collections often came to have an institutional as well as a personal character. The popes' collections were incorporated into the Bibliotheca Vaticana, and kings' libraries often evolved into national libraries. Over the centuries these were transformed from personal collections of fine books to multifaceted institutions serving the highest purposes of state and society. Many of the libraries assembled by doctors, lawyers, bankers, and merchant princes underwent the same transformation.

The Industrial Revolution and the expansive opportunities of 19th-century North America created a new set of rich men and women who were determined to enjoy their wealth. Some engaged in lavish displays of ostentation, some in philanthropy—and some, combining both impulses, began to collect paintings, sculpture, and fine books.

John Pierpont Morgan made his fortune from investment banking, railroads, and steel, and used it to assemble extraordinary collections of art and literature. His twenty-five-thousand-volume library emphasized beauty and rarity over intellectual importance, but it still had much to offer to scholars, who were admitted to the marble edifice that Morgan erected next to his midtown Manhattan home. His son dedicated the Morgan Library to the use of scholars, students, and book lovers.

Henry Edwards Huntington fell in love with California, where he had extensive real estate and electric railway interests. "The ownership of a fine library is the surest and swiftest way to immortality,"[34] he believed. To ensure that immortality, Huntington endowed an institution to preserve his library of English and American historical and literary documents forever. The library maintains its own research staff of distinguished scholars, and makes its books available to visiting scholars. It also sponsors conferences and publishes both documents from its collection and research studies of its materials.

◆ ◆ ◆

As far back as the Renaissance period, royal libraries served the needs of statecraft as well as the pleasures of princes. Mandatory deposit laws, introduced in 16th-century France, required that all books printed in the realm be sent to the royal collection. These laws not only ensured that the literary output of the country was gathered in a central location: they also simplified the process of keeping a watchful eye on what was being written and printed.

Ever since Charlemagne, the kings of France had maintained personal libraries, but it was not until the reign of Charles V in the 14th century that a true royal library came into being. Though it was established for the king's use, many of his successors allowed scholars to use it. In 1735 the Bibliothèque du Roi was permanently opened to the public, who were permitted to use the books twice a week.

From its medieval beginnings, the Bibliothèque du Roi grew steadily through the purchase of eminent private collections and its own acquisition efforts. French diplomats were instructed to procure books from the countries to which they were accredited. Missionaries and traders brought back books from the lands they visited. Duplicate books were exchanged with libraries in other countries; the king exchanged books with the emperor of China.

By the time of the French Revolution, the Bibliothèque du Roi had collected nearly two hundred thousand printed books and more than twenty-five thousand manuscripts. It was decreed a public library in the aftermath of the Revolution, and renamed the Bibliothèque Nationale. It was opened to students for four hours daily (on nine days out of every ten, the "decade" having temporarily replaced the week in the Revolutionary calendar) and to casual visitors on three out of every ten days. The collections were augmented with books confiscated from aristocrats executed or exiled, and from the resources of churches and monasteries. So many books were acquired in this way that fifty years later many remained "uncatalogued, unclassed, and even unstamped."[35] But these were not enough. Soon after the Revolution, the libraries of Europe were robbed of their treasures by Napoleon's armies. After Napoleon's downfall at Waterloo, most of these treasures were returned to their owners, but many remain still in the Bibliothèque Nationale.

♦ ♦ ♦

Like many other British institutions, the British Museum evolved more accidentally than purposefully. A handful of wealthy individuals collected historical documents, literary manuscripts, and scientific specimens, which were later given or sold to the nation. In his will, London physician Sir Hans Sloane offered his collections to the nation at a bargain price. Parliament had little money available, so a lottery was organized to raise the required twenty thousand pounds. This was used to buy the Sloane collections, and to endow a British Museum to house them along with other collections of historical documents. Just before the museum opened to the public in 1759, King George II presented it with the Royal Library. Its books and manuscripts had been collected by his predecessors since the reign of Edward IV.

In its early days, the British Museum was not a very lively place. It had very little money with which to buy books, so its growth depended almost entirely upon gifts. The aged physicians and clergymen who comprised its staff were seldom troubled by visitors; they regarded readers as a nuisance. But the museum soon outgrew its quarters, and a new building was designed in Bloomsbury, the home of the British Museum to this day.

When Antonio Panizzi was appointed Keeper of Printed Books in 1837, he insisted upon the rigorous enforcement of the mandatory deposit laws, which publishers had got into the habit of ignoring. He secured an appropriation of ten thousand pounds a year from Parliament for the purchase of books. And he improved both the physical facilities of the library and its staff, so that they might be adequate for the collection he meant to build: one that would not only possess "every book that was printed either by Englishmen or in English or relating to

England,"[36] but would also own "the best library of each language outside the native country of that language."[37]

By the end of Panizzi's tenure at the British Museum, the library's influence had spread far beyond London. American researchers used it regularly. Karl Marx based his scientific interpretation of history on the economic tracts and historical essays he read there while preparing *Das Kapital,* and Vladimir Ilyich Lenin found in the British Museum's collections not only revolutionary literature from Russia unavailable in his native land, but also documents from the English and French revolutions.

Other national libraries were not as easy to use. The British writer William Thackeray complained that in the Bibliothèque Nationale "the catalogue you consult is the librarian," who was always too busy to answer all of a reader's questions. "If I had to write on a French subject, the French Revolution for example, I would go to London for the books."[38] But he had an easier time of it than did J.G. Kohl, a German writer who had visited the Russian Imperial Library in St. Petersburg a few years earlier. "To get a book to read in the library itself is utterly impossible,"[39] he lamented, because of the cumbersome procedures required to request a title and the limited hours during which the library was open.

◆   ◆   ◆

In 1774, when the Continental Congress assembled in Philadelphia, it secured borrowing privileges from the Library Company of Philadelphia, with whom it shared Carpenter's Hall. After the Revolution, the new American government enjoyed access to the libraries of New York and Philadelphia. But in 1800 the national capital was moved to Washington, a new city that had no existing libraries.

A small library was established for the use of Congress, despite objections from people who felt that if congressmen were qualified to hold office, they would not need to learn their job from books at the taxpayers' expense. When British invaders burned the Capitol during the War of 1812, the three thousand volumes in that congressional library were dispersed or destroyed. Thomas Jefferson, who was deeply in debt, offered to sell his personal collection for whatever price the Congress saw fit to offer. It was one of the finest libraries in North America. With over six thousand volumes, its scope went well beyond narrowly defined legislative concerns. But Jefferson claimed that "I do not know that it contains any branch of science which Congress would wish to exclude from their collection; there is, in fact, no subject to which a Member of Congress may not have occasion to refer."[40] Though critics complained of the collection's unnecessarily broad scope, Congress narrowly voted to approve its purchase.

After the Civil War, the library began to seek out material basic to an understanding of American history, purchasing collections of manuscripts and early printed publications. As immigration and commerce increased America's concerns with events overseas, American embassies and consulates worldwide were asked to help in expanding the library's collection.

"There is, in fact, no subject to which a Member of Congress may not have occasion to refer." As the truth of Jefferson's words became ever clearer, a Legislative Reference Service was created, to provide congressmen and their staffs with information assembled from materials within the library. This was in keeping with the progressive spirit of the times, which advocated the application of scientific information to the solution of societal problems. Like its counterparts in state capitols, the Legislative Reference Service freed lawmakers from dependence upon lobbyists for information on proposed legislation and help in drafting bills.

Although it neither sought nor received any such official designation, the Library of Congress was becoming America's *de facto* national library. During the 1940s, Librarian of Congress Archibald MacLeish said that it was the responsibility of the Library of Congress to possess all library materials necessary to the Congress and to the officers of government of the United States in the performance of their duties; all books and other materials that express and record the life and achievements of the people of the United States; and the material parts of the records of other societies, past and present. But its wide-ranging collections were not the only reason that it has become the leading library in America.

Librarians knew there was no need for the same book to be cataloged in detail by every library that owned it. After all, the basic bibliographical details of the ordinary printed book—author, title, imprint, physical aspects—did not vary from one copy to another. Nor did its content. So the Library of Congress began selling copies of its printed catalog cards to other libraries. And, in turn, libraries contributed cataloging information for their books to a National Union Catalog maintained in Washington. By 1955 it contained more than thirteen million cards; eventually it was replaced by multivolume sets of catalog cards photographically reproduced, several cards to a page. In recent years this cataloging information has been produced on magnetic tapes and optical discs to make interactive searching by computer possible.

As the Library of Congress's collections grew from Thomas Jefferson's six thousand volumes to almost a million by the end of the 19th century, it outgrew the subject arrangement that had been inherited from Jefferson. The Dewey Decimal

Classification, which worked well in public and college library collections, was not detailed enough to reflect the contents of the Library of Congress. So the library devised its own classification, which has been adopted by large libraries across the United States and around the world.

Another area in which the Library of Congress has undertaken a leadership role on behalf of American libraries is that of the conservation and preservation of library materials. Though the invention of wood-pulp paper made possible the production of cheap books and newspapers, it imposed a limited life span on those publications. The rag paper used by the first printers has lasted for over five hundred years with little or no deterioration, but the chemicals used in wood-pulp paper provoke a gradual disintegration. The pages of a fifty- or hundred-year-old volume may crumble in its reader's hand. Librarians have microfilmed newspapers, laminated precious documents, and experimented with chemical technology for removing or neutralizing the destructive acids from pulp paper. The Library of Congress has been in the forefront of this work, conducting chemical research and using innovative computer techniques to preserve and distribute rare pictures and documents.

The Library of Congress is still, in the letter of the law, an agency designed to serve the legislative branch of the United States government. But it has become in fact the American national library, and is becoming one of the cornerstones of the evolving worldwide research library system.

· 8 ·

Colleges and Universities

B y 1700 the universities of Europe had become strong-
holds of orthodoxy, playing little role in the enhancement
of knowledge. To anyone other than a future clergyman,
they had almost nothing to offer. Doctors and lawyers could
learn their art by apprenticeship, and a banker or merchant did
not need a university education.

Like their parent institutions, university libraries contributed little to intellectual life. Although the 16th and 17th
centuries produced masterworks of imaginative literature, the
writings of Shakespeare, Cervantes, and Molière were not studied in universities or collected by their libraries. The scientific
writings of Copernicus and Galileo, of Harvey and Newton—
all were ignored by the university curriculum and the libraries
that existed to support it.

But people whose horizons had been expanded by the
Renaissance and the Reformation began to rethink the idea of
education and of the university. They envisioned an institution
that would prepare young men for careers in the new world
that was unfolding around them.

The University of Göttingen opened in 1737 in a small town
a few miles from the German city of Hannover. Göttingen was

intended to be a research university as well as a teaching institution: a community in which knowledge would be added to the store of humankind as well as transmitted from one generation to another. This would not be possible without a strong, well-developed library, and Göttingen owed much of its reputation—by the end of the century it was esteemed the leading university of the German-speaking world—to the care with which its library was conceived and organized.

Christian Gottlob Heyne, Göttingen's chief librarian for nearly fifty years, believed that "the number of books is that which counts least." He called for a working library whose books would "illuminate the art and taste, not only of one country, but all educated nations."[41] The steady, careful selection of the best new publications made Göttingen the best university library in Europe.

The medieval university library had required its treasures to be used on site. By the end of the 18th century, readers were expected to use library books in their homes. Printed books could be more easily and cheaply replaced than manuscripts. The university library was an uninviting place in which to spend any substantial period of time. The damp and cold were seldom allayed by stoves, for fear of fire. The same consideration kept lamps out of libraries. December's daylight lasts only eight hours in northern Europe, so it is little wonder that many libraries curtailed their hours in winter.

❖ ❖ ❖

North America lacked the abundance of opportunities for professional training that existed in Europe. American colleges educated physicians, lawyers, and men of business as well as ministers of the Gospel. At all the colleges founded in America before the Revolution, libraries were accorded central importance. Samuel Davies, president of the College of New Jersey at Princeton, wrote that "a large and well assorted collection of books...is the most ornamental and useful furniture of a College, and the most proper and valuable fund with which it can be endowed."[42]

American college libraries were small. During the colonial period the largest collection, at Harvard, contained fewer than fifteen thousand volumes. Most colleges owned between one and three thousand. Despite their small size, these collections were adequate to support the curriculum, which emphasized theology and the classics, and to provide students with access to the best of English literature.

Most colleges occupied a single building in their early years, in which the library was most commonly located on the second floor, above the chapel. A large, centrally located room, it was also used as the site of trustees' meetings, dinners for eminent guests, and commencement gatherings. These activities did not interfere with library operations, for college libraries were open to students only a couple of hours each week.

While library rules permitted only limited access to books, this did not greatly disadvantage students. Well into the 19th century, college instruction in America relied more upon the textbook than upon the library. Students read standard introductory works on philosophy, mathematics, and the classics, demonstrating their absorption of this material through classroom recitation. Neither original thought nor creative synthesis was required. Science and modern languages were considered less important, and law and medicine were rarely taught in colleges.

But the curriculum changed to reflect the needs of an industrial society, and libraries changed with it. By the end of the 19th century most college libraries in America were open six or seven days a week, from morning to night. Large reading rooms and extensive reference collections accommodated students working in the library building, which improvements in heating, lighting, and ventilation made a more attractive place in which to read or study. Students were allowed to borrow books to read at home or in their fraternity houses or dormitories.

⬩ ⬩ ⬩

During the 19th century, Germany became the world's leader in science and scholarship. Following Göttingen's example, the German university was transformed into a center for the discovery of new knowledge and the development of students' intellectual capabilities. A leading instrument in this process was the seminar. A small group of students, working under the guidance of their professor, solved research problems that required them to work with original source materials and to learn and use the tools of scholarship in their discipline. The traditional closed-stack central library, in which readers were required to choose their books from catalogs instead of selecting them from the shelves, could not support this level of intellectual activity.

The seminar demanded a new sort of library, one in which a wide range of publications was placed in the hands of professor and student alike, without barriers between the book and its reader. An American scholar who had studied in Germany described the seminar library as "a well-lighted, well-equipped comfortable place for study and research" where "each member has a key to the room and comes and goes as he pleases.…The room is accessible at all hours during the day and evening, and is usually an attractive place for quiet, uninterrupted work."[43] In many cases books in the seminar libraries came from the professors' private collections. Books were not expensive in Germany, and it was not unusual for a scholar to own a working library of ten or twenty thousand volumes.

In France, Spain, and Italy many university libraries were housed in outmoded buildings, with inadequate seating for readers and insufficient space to house the collections. In the stacks, books often stood two or three deep on the shelves. Bookshelves overflowed into attics, cellars, and corridors. Boxes and packets of uncataloged books, theses, and pamphlets were stored wherever room could be found for them. Catalogues were inadequate, staff insufficient, and library hours limited. To this day, admits a French historian, libraries are "one of the weak points of our universities."[44]

❖ ❖ ❖

During the early years of the 20th century, a small number of universities both in America and in Europe trained the bulk of higher degree recipients. As the demand for scientists and professionals trained to the doctoral level increased, more institutions began to offer graduate-level instruction. This led to a vast expansion of academic libraries throughout the Western world, and to a similarly great expansion of the scope of academic library collections.

As knowledge accumulated in printed form, and in an increasing number of nonprint media, it was impossible for even the most affluent and ambitious library to collect everything. As this became more widely realized, various schemes were instituted to ensure that scholars might have access to materials that could not be collected by their home institution. German universities adopted such a plan in the aftermath of World War I, when there was little money available for library acquisitions. Bonn bought books on Romance philology and literature; Göttingen, English; and so forth, with nine academic libraries taking part in the scheme.

In America the Farmington Plan brought together several dozen major academic libraries who agreed to divide up responsibility for collecting all new foreign books and pamphlets "that might reasonably be expected to interest a research worker in the United States."[45] The Midwest Inter-Library Center—now the Center for Research Libraries—collected old college catalogs, foreign dissertations, and outdated textbooks. These could be consulted by visitors, or mailed to member libraries for use by their readers.

Resource sharing among libraries also came into vogue. Standards for interlibrary loan were adopted by library associations, with national libraries usually serving as lender of last resort. To facilitate this, union catalogs were established to show the holdings of participating libraries. The National Union Catalog, maintained by the Library of Congress in Washington, was distributed in card form to over a hundred major American libraries and principal libraries abroad. The *Union List of Serials*, published in five massive volumes, listed thousands of journals and the libraries in which they might be found. It was purchased by most of the major libraries of North America.

More recently, the development of online public-access catalogs has made the holdings of libraries worldwide accessible to scholars on distant continents. But this is not the same thing as providing access to the contents of these collections. Despite claims that anyone with a computer and a modem can "browse through the Library of Congress," very few library resources are actually available for reading online. There is still a tremendous gap between knowing that a particular book exists in a particular library, and being able to see its contents on the computer display screen.

In the developing countries, universities and university libraries are much more limited in resources. Books and journals from the developed world are often too expensive to purchase, and tropical climates are hard on library collections. Thus it is difficult for developing countries to train the leaders they need, and many of those who go to Europe or America to study do not return.

12. Circular Reading Room of the British Museum Library—Soon after it opened in 1857, the *Illustrated London News* printed this drawing of Antonio Panizzi's magnificent reading room. Although the British Library has recently moved to new quarters next door to the St. Pancras railway station, the Circular Reading Room will continue to serve visitors to the British Museum in Bloomsbury.

13. Reading Room of the Boston Public Library in 1871 — "Rich and poor assemble together and alike in this narrow dispensary, and a great many of them too." This wood-engraving by J.J. Harley from a contemporary magazine shows the popularity of America's first urban public library. (Courtesy of the Print Department, Boston Public Library)

14. General Reading Room, Gorbals Branch, Glasgow Public Library. The Gorbals was a working-class district in Scotland's largest city. This branch library, the first in the city, shared a building with a public bathhouse. (From *Descriptive Handbook of the Glasgow Corporation Public Libraries*, 1907)

15. Student Working at a Computer Terminal— The Sedgwick Branch of the New York Public Library opened in 1994. Like most modern American public libraries, it offers visitors computer equipment as well as more traditional library services. (Photo by David Grossman, courtesy of the New York Public Library)

16. The Stacks of the New York Public Library at 42nd Street—This cutaway drawing appeared on the cover of the *Scientific American*. It shows the immense resources placed at the disposal of those who flocked to the library's reading rooms. The stacks were (and are) closed to the public, who requested and collected their books at the delivery desk shown at the top left, and read them in the spacious room visible through the delivery desk windows. (*Scientific American*, May 27, 1911)

17. Main Reading Room of the New York Public Library at 42nd Street—The newly renovated Rose Main Reading Room retains the library's original bronze lamps and oak tables, but today those tables are wired for data as well as electricity, and many of them hold computer workstations. (Photo copyright James Rudnick, courtesy of the New York Public Library)

18. Children's Reading Room at Hull House, Chicago—Hull House was a settlement house founded by pioneer social worker Jane Addams to help newcomers learn how to cope with the problems and opportunities of city life. The Chicago Public Library opened a small branch here, to serve the children who came to Hull House. (Courtesy of Jane Addams Memorial Collection, Special Collections, University Library, University of Illinois at Chicago)

19. The New Library of Alexandria—With the support of the international community and the Egyptian government, the University of Alexandria is attempting to recapture the glory of the ancient library. The new Biblioteca Alexandrina is being built on what is thought to be the same site that its predecessor occupied two thousand years ago. Intended to take its place among the major research libraries of the world, it will assemble millions of volumes representing the learning of all nations and cultures. (Architect's model, from *Aramco World*, March/April 1994, by permission of the publishers)

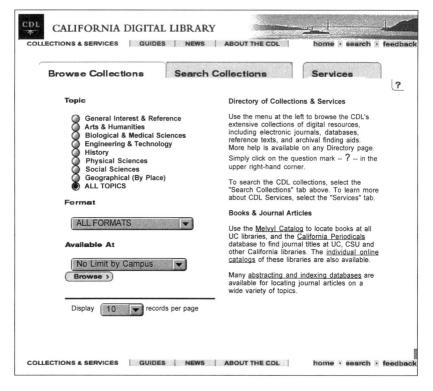

20. California Digital Library—The California Digital Library offers an alternative model of the research library of the future. A project of the University of California, it is intended to make a wide range of virtual resources available to students and faculty at the University's nine campuses. Unlike the other University libraries, it is not a collection of books, but a collection of access points to computer files of information. This screen shot from the CDL website suggests the scope of the material available to the University community. (Image used with permission of the University of California; copyright 1999 The Regents of the University of California.)

·9·

The People's Libraries

The Protestant Reformation gave birth to the idea that every member of society must have at least enough education to read the Bible. With the spread of democracy, an educated populace became as much a necessity in the political as in the religious sphere. In Gutenberg's time, there were very few in Europe who were able to read, and most of them did their reading in Latin. But by 1800, at least in the Protestant countries of northern Europe, over half the adult population could read simple texts in their native language. These numbers do not tell the whole story. The audience for books was multiplied by the practice of reading aloud, within the household and among workmates and neighbors.

As the number of readers and the taste for reading increased, the book trade grew likewise. Booksellers multiplied, and magazines devoted to book reviewing emerged. But books were expensive; few people could afford to buy all the books they desired to read. Just because books were too costly to buy did not mean that they must be too costly to read. By the 18th century, French and British booksellers allowed people to read books in their shops for a small fee, and rented them for home reading. London coffeehouses provided newspapers and magazines for their customers, and sold reading privileges by the hour to those who did not want coffee or beer. Subscription reading rooms offered middle-class readers access to published news and comment in more genteel surroundings, while aristocrats enjoyed the reading facilities of their clubs.

In 1730, a young printer in Philadelphia named Benjamin Franklin organized a subscription library, and ordered books from England. These included titles on mathematics and natural science as well as Homer and Vergil, contemporary magazines such as *The Tatler* and *The Spectator*, and practical works such as Daniel Defoe's *Compleat English Tradesman* and Philip Miller's *Gardener's Dictionary*. The Library Company of Philadelphia was imitated throughout British North America, especially in the New England colonies. The Redwood Library of Newport, Rhode Island, and the New York Society Library each owned nearly a thousand books at the beginning of the Revolution. By 1780 there were fifty-one "social libraries" in New England alone.

Those who did not subscribe to a social library might borrow books from a commercial circulating library. These were maintained by many booksellers, dry goods merchants, and other businessmen who saw them as a profitable sideline that would increase traffic through their shop doors. The bulk of their collection was fiction, though most attempted to maintain titles covering a wide range of interests. But there was more money in novels than in sermons.

Mudie's Select Library brought respectability to the industry. Charles Edward Mudie offered his middle-class customers in Britain both the convenience of access to an immense collection of current books and the assurance that nothing they might find at Mudie's would cause the slightest embarrassment when read aloud within the family circle. For two-thirds of the price of a single novel, Mudie's customers could have their choice of current fiction—not to mention a wide range of non-fiction books—for an entire year.

Those English readers who were unable to pay the subscription fees of the private circulating libraries were served, if they were served at all, by the small libraries established by the Society for Promoting Christian Knowledge and the Religious Tract Society. These collections of one hundred volumes or so were kept in churches, chapels, and schools. Though there were several thousand of them, they had little to offer the working-class reader. Their books were almost entirely religious in nature, as were those of the "itinerating libraries" that served rural regions. As competition to the tavern for the scarce spare time of the tired workingman they were extremely ineffective.

◆ ◆ ◆

The Public Libraries Act of 1850 was one of many social reforms undertaken by Great Britain as a response to the rapid growth of urban centers after the Industrial Revolution. It allowed (but did not require) cities to create public libraries and expend tax money on their maintenance. Few cities did so; in many, proposals to fund public libraries were repeatedly and overwhelmingly defeated. This was not only because it would increase taxes. Some voters felt that the provision of libraries should be left to private organizations. Others, distrustful of any increase in the spread of popular education, saw the public library as a source of political agitation.

Even where public libraries were established, they were rarely supported properly. After a building was provided, there was seldom enough money left to buy books or pay staff adequate wages. Without a good, well-balanced book collection, people were not likely to use the library. Both its supporters and its opponents regarded the British public library as an educational and cultural program for the working classes—and therein lay its essential difference from the public library in America.

Though other New England towns had used tax money to support libraries, Boston was the first American city to decide that a public library was an essential aspect of modern urban life, one that should be established and maintained by the municipal government. It was not surprising that the New England states were the leaders in the founding of public libraries, just as they were in the establishment of free public education. Their economy increasingly depended upon manufacturing and commerce, which required a well-educated labor force. The religious sentiments of New England's business leaders inspired the foundation of numerous charitable institutions. A strong sense of civic pride encouraged the formation of public libraries. And public libraries offered many social advantages. They would help to keep working people away from the taverns and also provide mechanics and clerks with the tools to upgrade their skills. The availability of books on agriculture, technology, geography, and commerce would increase the prosperity of the commonwealth, by making its citizens more efficient at their several vocations. And a public library would help to attract migration and investment to its community.

Library users included professional men, artisans, and those in "mercantile callings": clerks, salesmen, merchants, and bookkeepers were heavily represented among those who thronged the reading rooms. With few other educational opportunities open to them, women were among the most enthusiastic users of public libraries. "Rich and poor assemble together and alike in this narrow dispensary, and a great many of them too,"[46] boasted the Boston Public Library, which counted bartenders, wood choppers, and washerwomen among its users. Fiction was by far the most popular category of reading. While many librarians disliked it, they hoped that providing fiction would attract readers whose taste could be improved. Among nonfiction books, the most frequently consulted or borrowed were history, biography, and travel. Scientific and technical works were well used by ambitious young readers.

Other regions of the country were slower than the New England states to establish public libraries. While the Boston Public Library opened its doors in 1854, it was not until 1879 that the New York Free Circulating Library came into existence. Privately founded, it did not receive municipal funding for the first seven years of its existence. Many New York leaders believed that libraries were a charitable enterprise rather than an essential municipal service.

This attitude was vigorously opposed by Andrew Carnegie, who believed that in a democratic society government must assume responsibility for providing education at all levels. Carnegie, born of poor Scottish parents, made a colossal fortune in the steel industry. He gave millions of dollars for the construction of public library buildings in the United States and the British Empire, but only on the condition that the municipality receiving the gift guarantee to establish and maintain the library with annual appropriations of public money. Carnegie's offer convinced many cities to institute tax-supported libraries rather than wait for some benefactor to endow one.

• • •

In the larger cities of Great Britain and America, public libraries contained separate reference and circulating collections, both of which were housed in closed stacks. Readers would choose books from a printed catalog; many libraries required that ten or a dozen selections be made in case the first choice was unavailable. Request slips would be handed in at the counter, and library assistants would retrieve the books from the stacks and hand them over the counter to the reader.

Much of the library's space would be devoted to a large reading room, where books from the reference collection could be used. This benefited working people, who often could not afford the light and heat that would enable them to read books in their dismal living quarters. Gin was cheap and beer was cheaper, which made the public house or corner saloon a serious rival to the public library. Librarians knew that they had to offer more than the loan of books if they were to entice the working classes. For the same reason, public libraries were open late into the evening (especially as electric lighting came into use) and on Sundays. Many cities established branch libraries to bring books closer to their expanding residential neighborhoods.

With the improvement of working-class educational and housing conditions, the nature of reference collections changed. They increasingly catered to the needs of students and specialists, who consulted them for detailed information on commerce, industry, or local history. Lending collections accounted for an increasing proportion of library resources. The space devoted to reading rooms shrank as library design came to emphasize open access to the book collection. As readers gained direct access to books, a better system was needed for finding those they wanted. This was provided by the card catalog, which could be kept up-to-date more easily and cheaply than a printed catalog in book form, and the Dewey Decimal System, which provided a logical and flexible way of arranging books by subject.

The mere provision of books and catalogs was not enough. As encyclopedias, indexes, and directories became widely available, libraries increasingly offered their patrons help in finding answers to their questions, where these were contained in books in the library's collection. This "reference service" was improved by the practice of dividing large public library collections into subject departments, staffed with librarians whose training and experience qualified them as subject specialists.

Public libraries and librarians, like teachers and clergymen, saw themselves as upholders of the established order. Their educational and social mission was to enable men and women to rise within society as currently constituted, not to provide them with the intellectual tools to overthrow it. Radical literature was seldom to be found on library shelves. Many critics had even opposed the provision of newspapers in libraries because their availability might encourage political agitation.

But by the 1930s, librarians came to cherish diversity of opinion and free access to the widest possible range of viewpoints. Opposition to censorship has become a central part of the librarian's professional ethics. Public libraries have often come under attack for making unpopular publications available. Libraries today are among the strongest defenders of freedom of the press and of intellectual freedom in general. In 1939 the United States celebrated the 150th anniversary of the Bill of Rights, the ten amendments that enshrined the basic freedoms of American citizens in the newly adopted federal constitution. In that year the American Library Association proclaimed a "Library Bill of Rights," which has served as the model for similar policy statements in several other countries.

❖ ❖ ❖

In continental Europe, the establishment of public libraries lagged behind developments in the English-speaking countries. The European educational system emphasized the preparation of young men for their life's work rather than the production of an informed citizenry. And readers were accustomed to owning books rather than borrowing them, a practice encouraged by the comparatively low price of books on the continent.

In many countries of 19th-century Europe, illiteracy was high and educational opportunities limited. Even in the more literate countries of western Europe, public libraries served only a small number of people. Municipal libraries were concerned with preserving the nation's literary heritage, not with accommodating the needs of the reading public. Even in those libraries founded specifically for the use of the common people, the book collections reflected the literary standards of intellectuals and cultural bureaucrats rather than the tastes of ordinary readers. Books were chosen more for their conformity to approved political or religious doctrine than for their popular appeal. Serious literature rather than entertaining fiction was the rule. Even as late as 1952 an American visitor observed that "one simply does not find mystery stories and the like in the Parisian public libraries."[47] Subscription fees were often charged, which discouraged poor families from using the public libraries.

Working people turned to newsstands and commercial lending libraries for their reading matter, or to privately operated libraries. Many industrial companies provided libraries for their employees. Religious societies played a major role in bringing library service to small towns and rural areas. But in totalitarian societies, governments found a use for public libraries: to shape the thinking of their citizens.

Two years after the Russian Revolution, the citizens of Petrograd were encouraged to use public libraries: "As the proletarian revolution wants you to be sober and clear minded you should not fail to obtain a book at your local library."[48] Lenin himself was a strong believer in the value of libraries. In 1913 he wrote admiringly of Western countries that "see the pride and glory of the public library not in the number of rarities it possesses...but in the extent to which books circulate among the people."[49]

Public libraries, like other aspects of education, were seen as vehicles for the advancement of the Communist Party and the Soviet state. Their role, according to Lenin, was to "educate the public strictly towards a revolutionary outlook and revolutionary action."[50] When the party leadership changed, or the party's teachings were revised, librarians removed books whose contents were now unacceptable, or cut out offending pages. In support of their role in fighting illiteracy and encouraging worker self-education, Soviet public libraries provided extensive advisory services to their readers. This also enabled libraries to steer their readers toward those books that enjoyed the favor of the party.

Like the Soviet Union, Nazi Germany saw the public library as a vehicle for the penetration of the ruling party's values into every aspect of society. To this end, the Nazis vastly increased the number of public libraries in Germany, and established libraries in border areas. The concept of "the German folk" could be strengthened by increasing the hold of the German language on border populations, and the provision of German books was recognized as a powerful means to that end.

Although public libraries on the American model had been founded in Berlin and a few other German cities, these were neither free nor tax-supported. Upper- and middle-class Germans were accustomed to buying their own books. Thus public libraries were associated with a working-class clientele, who also patronized the subscription libraries operated as sidelines by newsstands and tobacconists. Perhaps for this reason,

German librarians considered advising readers the most important of their professional activities. Public libraries did not have open stacks; catalogs were difficult to use and seldom entirely up-to-date. The librarian served as mediator between book and reader, guiding his selections from the carefully chosen collection of serious books.

This tradition made it easy to incorporate the public library into the Nazi program for the transformation of German society. Books by Jewish writers, communists, and others hated by the Nazis were removed from library collections, while lists of Nazi-approved titles were distributed to librarians. Even the library catalogs were revised to reflect Nazi views on race and nationalism.

◆ ◆ ◆

After World War II, educational opportunities expanded across North America and western Europe. Cheap paperback books enabled ordinary people to build their own home libraries. Television gave millions of people the opportunity to travel vicariously around the world, and brought a wide variety of both light and serious entertainment into the home.

At first these developments reduced the importance of the public library as a source of knowledge and entertainment. It was seldom thought of as "the people's university," a role now bestowed upon educational television and innovative institutions of higher education. But public libraries changed in response to their changing surroundings. They learned television programs often stimulated demand for the books from which they had been adapted. Many of the students at newly established schools and colleges found the public library a convenient place to study. And readers were no longer limited to the books owned by their local libraries. Through participation in regional networks, member libraries were able to call upon the resources of university collections and national libraries.

The most recent developments in access to information, the global Internet and its descendant the World Wide Web, offer another opportunity to the public library. By providing public access to the worldwide computer network, and advice in selecting from the countless information sources available in cyberspace, public libraries are in fact returning to their original functions.

· 10 ·

Libraries for Young People

The idea of providing libraries for the use of young readers was a long time in coming. In much of 19th-century Europe, illiteracy was still widespread. Even when a child's parents could read, in many a household the only books were a Bible, a prayer book, and an almanac. It was in America, where an educated population was essential to both the political and religious foundations of society, that the first substantial efforts to provide libraries for young readers were made.

The Boston Public Library's founders conceived it as "the crowning glory of our system of City Schools."[51] Because the first public libraries saw themselves as agencies for enabling school graduates to continue the educational process on their own, they directed their collections and services to adults. Some displayed signs warning "children and dogs not admitted," and most libraries refused entry to anyone under fourteen years of age. Books were not lent for home use; the reference and reading rooms were crowded with adult users. It was not until the 1890s that public libraries really began to serve children.

The problems of urban life convinced social reformers that children needed wholesome alternatives to the street-corner and saloon. Child labor came under increasing regulation, and compulsory education laws were more stringently enforced.

The number of children with both the ability and the leisure time to read increased substantially. In response to this, public libraries began to make service to children a high priority, offering reading rooms and lending services. These were often staffed by young women, who were thought to have a special aptitude for work with children.

After World War I, public library service to children became widespread, and was extended even to those who were too young to read. To encourage preschool children to find enjoyment in books, libraries offered picture book collections and story hours. Films, puppet programs, and other activities enticed children and their parents into the library. For older readers there were book discussion groups, hobby programs, and visits from writers. The books themselves became more appealing, as librarians encouraged inviting covers and attractive illustrations. Because libraries represented a substantial portion of the market for children's literature, publishers were eager to oblige.

In Great Britain, where middle-class reformers sought to use libraries to turn potential delinquents into useful members of society, children's services became almost universal. By the end of the 1930s, separate children's rooms were common. Story hours and other special programs were offered to attract children to the library. In both Britain and America, as in Canada, Australia, and New Zealand, service to children has become one of the leading purposes of the public library.

Outside the English-speaking countries, libraries were much slower to extend their services to young readers. In the industrial cities of 19th-century Germany, a few public libraries offered children's programs and reading rooms intended to help keep idle youngsters out of trouble. The German view of librarianship emphasized rigid standards of book selection, and a strong role for the librarian in advising readers. In many

German libraries it was the father of the family who held the library card and selected the reading matter for the entire household.

Before World War I, the only children's libraries in France were small collections distributed to primary schools. These resided in locked cupboards except on the rare occasions at which books were distributed. In 1924 a group of American women opened a model children's library in Paris. Patterned on the American public library, l'Heure Joyeuse offered children and young teenagers a selection of attractive books on open shelves, a program of story hours and book discussions, and an opportunity to participate in the day-to-day operation of the library. It was extremely successful, and influenced library service to adults as well as to young people.

Since the end of World War II, library service to young people in western Europe has followed the Anglo-American pattern. Well-chosen collections, placed on open shelves, are intended to accustom children and adolescents to read for pleasure, with the goal of making reading a lifelong habit.

The Soviet Union had extensive networks of children's libraries and youth libraries, operated separately from the public libraries serving adults. In addition, trade unions, youth clubs, and other organizations provided library services. More than one hundred fifty thousand school libraries served educational needs. All this was intended to support the "development of the personality"[52] of Soviet youth along communist lines and "the formation of the Marxist-Leninist concept of the world."[53] Libraries worked to instil in children good reading habits, so that they could play their parts as workers and as citizens in Soviet society. Librarians paid careful attention to advising them on their choice of reading, and discussed books with children when they returned them.

In most of Asia, Africa, and Latin America, there were until recently few young readers to be served by libraries. In many of these countries, educational opportunities were limited to the children of upper- and middle-class families. Even where an attempt was made to provide a primary education to the masses, the resources seldom existed to fund widespread library services.

◆   ◆   ◆

Adolescents as well as younger children worried 19th-century reformers. The middle-class mind found it easy to imagine the vice and depravity that lay ahead of the unguided working-class youngster. Teenage workers were encouraged to use public libraries for self-improvement. Indeed, one of the reasons advanced to encourage business support for them was that they would enable ambitious youngsters to learn what they needed to advance in their trades or careers. Recreational reading was encouraged less as an end in itself than as a desirable alternative to the poolroom or the saloon.

By the 1930s in America and most of Europe, a boy or girl in the middle teen years was expected to be in school rather than in the work place. High schools increasingly had libraries of their own, often duplicating the facilities and resources of public libraries. The public library's service to this age group evolved into a supplement to the school curriculum and a provider of recreational reading. With the increasing sophistication of young people, there was an increasing tendency to provide teenagers with practically unlimited access to the adult collections. Special resources, ranging from a designated bookshelf in a small library to an entire branch of the New York Public Library system, were provided to accommodate their particular interests and concerns.

Many libraries changed the nature of their service to young people. They placed less emphasis on traditional book-centered programs—book talks, book discussion groups, literary magazines—and more emphasis on subject-oriented activities based on a broader conception of adolescents' information needs. But most teenagers in the affluent West have many other things to do than read books, and see little reason to use public libraries except when school assignments require it.

Changing trends in teaching methods and the increasing availability of well-written books for children provoked an interest in extending library service to children in their schools. In early days, the one-room schoolhouse gave many children all the formal education they were ever to receive, and even those who went beyond the primary level studied a narrow range of subjects. When an entire classroom worked from a single textbook, there was little need for school libraries. But as the curriculum became more diversified, and greater attention was paid to the individual needs of students, the need arose for access to wider book collections.

Many public libraries established branches in school buildings, while others lent books in large numbers to teachers for classroom reading. It was not until after World War II that libraries became common in American primary schools. The launch of the first artificial earth satellite by the Soviet Union in 1957 aroused American concern for the adequacy of the nation's schools, and for their libraries. Within twenty-five years, five out of every six elementary schools had a library or media center, and a high school without a library was nearly unthinkable.

❖ ❖ ❖

Public and school libraries have had a major influence on the development of children's literature. Librarians choosing books for their collections have attempted to balance the desirability of the content with the appeal of the books to young readers. They have also sought to exert a larger influence on the books available to children and adolescents. Awards such as the American Library Association's John Newbery Medal not only recognize excellence in children's writing but also provide a strong financial incentive for the production of good books. Awards are proudly proclaimed on the covers of winning books, and sales to schools, libraries, booksellers, and parents usually rise substantially.

Librarians have had less of an impact on adult reading. The early public librarians aspired to provide an uplifting influence upon their communities and to guide the reading of adults bent upon self-improvement and self-culture. But the availability of good cheap paperback books, cultural and educational programs on radio and television, and vastly expanded access to higher education provided many alternatives to the public library's role in adult education.

In developing countries the public library still fulfills much of the role envisioned by the library pioneers of England and America. Poverty and lack of other educational opportunities make libraries attractive to ambitious youths and adults. In most of these countries public libraries, where they exist at all, are confined to the national capital or the largest cities. Book collections are small, and their contents outdated. The heavy use they receive wears them out quickly. Few publications are available in the national languages, and even today library collections are heavily Western in content.

Readers in rural areas, if they receive any library service at all, get their books through the mail or borrow them from small collections deposited at local schools or health centers. In many African countries book shipments are sent by rail or truck or river boat; or library vans, equipped with makeshift accommodation for their staff, travel from village to village on circuits that might take several weeks.

Often the only libraries accessible to the public are those maintained by foreign governments: the United States Information Agency, the British Council, the Alliance Française. These seldom lend books, but that hardly matters: for many who live in the crowded housing of teeming cities, a quiet place to read is almost as important as the reading matter itself. The welcome for these libraries was not a unanimous one. The United States Information Agency was seen by some as a front for the Central Intelligence Agency, and its library activities viewed with suspicion by those inclined to doubt American motives. USIA libraries were often attacked during anti-American protest demonstrations, testimony to their symbolic importance.

◆　◆　◆

At the end of the 20th century, it has become apparent that children will spend their adult lives in a world substantially different from that into which they were born. The role of the school and public library has been to help young people to equip themselves to face that uncertain future. Those who feel that young people require more rather than less guidance in making decisions tend to look with disfavor on the availability of books that advocate ideas or portray situations that do not conform to their desired norms. Those who believe that young people should have access to the information they need to form their own opinions naturally encourage the widest possible representation of viewpoints in the library collection and the widest possible provision of library service. The tension between these attitudes is proof of the importance of library service to young people.

· 11 ·

Libraries at Work

As geographical and scientific knowledge grew, so did the number of professions devoted to their application. The Industrial Revolution made human activities more dependent upon technology, and the advance of technology was increasingly dependent upon the exchange of information. Knowledge that had once been transferred by word of mouth now needed to be recorded, preserved, and transmitted in a more organized manner. To organize the literature of science and technology, specialized libraries came into being. But although the term "special library" came into use at the beginning of the 20th century, to describe libraries dedicated to serving a particular clientele rather than the general public, the idea of the special library goes back thousands of years.

•   •   •

Medical literature is almost as old as writing itself. The ancient Egyptians had surgical textbooks, Hippocrates and Galen codified the medical knowledge of the Greeks, and monastic botanists of the Middle Ages compiled books on herbs and drugs. As the scientific method began to be applied to medicine and surgery, doctors learned their trade in the laboratory and the library. When they entered practice, they assembled private libraries, and joined together to found medical societies that often collected books and journals for the use of their members.

The world's greatest medical library, the National Library of Medicine, began as a small collection of books in the office of the Surgeon General of the United States Army. This officer supervised physicians and surgeons at army posts across the country, and was responsible for providing them with essential journals and reference works. In 1865 a young assistant surgeon named John Shaw Billings was placed in charge of the medical library.

At first it was only a spare-time job, but Billings soon became an enthusiastic collector of medical literature. He solicited current subscriptions and back issues from medical editors and publishers across the country and in Europe. He enlisted a network of physicians to locate and obtain obscure material for him, encouraging them to visit retired colleagues and doctors' widows in pursuit of medical literature. To obtain foreign publications, Billings wrote to American diplomats in other countries, as well as missionaries and other American physicians residing abroad.

After the Civil War the Surgeon General's Library was opened to civilian as well as military readers. To make the contents of the library more accessible, Billings began a subject index of its periodical collection. By the summer of 1875 he and his assistants had prepared tens of thousands of index cards. Not all of this work was done at the library. Volunteers, ranging from bored Army surgeons at sleepy frontier posts to a bedridden Confederate general, were supplied with journals to index and a list of subject terms to use. The resulting *Index-Catalogue of the Surgeon-General's Library* was an enormous listing of "everything which contains either a new fact, a new idea, or a new way of stating old ones."[54] Four years later another publication, *Index Medicus*, began to offer "a monthly classified record of the current medical literature of the world."

Ever since, the library's role as the world's leading medical bibliographer has been even more important than its status as the world's largest collection of medical literature. In 1956 it was placed under civilian management as the National Library of Medicine, and began exploring new ways of bringing doctors and information together. Early experiments with computerized indexing led to the establishment of MEDLINE, an electronic index to current medical literature. Doctors and scientists no longer needed to consult the bulky volumes of *Index Medicus* to identify the papers they wanted to read, and the ability to combine search commands made it possible to locate material with a precision previously unattainable.

With the spread of computers into offices and homes, it became possible for individuals, whether health professionals or members of the public, to use these services. The library developed software that simplified the search process and allowed readers to order copies of journal articles by computer, and used the World Wide Web to make these widely available. The pioneering role established for the library by John Shaw Billings continues into the 21st century.

❖ ❖ ❖

Of all human institutions, the law relies the most upon written documents. Ever since Hammurabi proclaimed the laws of Babylon, lawgivers have prepared codes setting forth all the regulations governing persons and property and their relations to each other and to society at large.

Continental Europe derived its legal system from Roman

civil law. Statutes enacted by legislatures in Civil Law countries are much more important than the records of cases previously decided by judges. In countries whose legal system was based on the Common Law of England—that is, in most of the English-speaking world—lawyers and judges do not find the law by consulting the statute books. Instead, they search the published reports of previously decided legal cases to find precedents applicable to the situation at hand. These decisions are binding on judges considering future cases, unless they are overturned by statute, and serve as the basis for the legal advice rendered by attorneys to their clients. This means that a large collection of case law is essential to the modern lawyer.

Today's law libraries are managed by librarians trained in both librarianship and the law, who help lawyers search the legal literature more effectively. They rely heavily upon electronic indexes and databases. Like doctors, lawyers make tremendously important decisions based on the information they find in their professional libraries. They are willing to pay the cost of information, if they can get it quickly and reliably when they need it.

· · ·

In the industrialized countries of the world, most major commercial and manufacturing enterprises maintain library services. They are expected to pay for themselves by making managers and workers directly concerned with the primary functions of the firm—design, production, marketing—more effective in the performance of their daily work. A leading purpose of the industrial library is to avoid spending money to duplicate research that is already available.

Many professional societies and trade associations maintain libraries and information bureaus. In addition to collecting the specialized literature of their fields, these groups often operate abstracting and indexing services. These provide brief summaries of important new publications, which can be used to keep aware of new developments and to identify publications containing useful information. This form of institutional cooperation among competitors serves not only their own information needs but also helps academic, governmental, and other users.

Patents are issued by governments to encourage inventors, by granting them a monopoly on the sale or use of their inventions for a limited period of time. To evaluate patent applications, a patent examiner needs to understand the existing state of the art and the extent to which the proposed invention surpasses it. For this purpose, the patent offices of industrial nations established libraries of technological publications. As patent office collections grew in size and importance, their value to those outside the patent field was recognized. In Britain, the Patent Office Library evolved into the National Reference Library of Science and Invention, and became a part of the British Library when the latter became independent of the British Museum.

Patent offices are not the only government agencies to maintain extensive libraries. Even when a great national library exists in the capital city, most executive agencies have libraries of their own. Some of these, such as the library of the Foreign and Commonwealth Office in London or the Department of the Interior in Washington, are among the world's greatest collections in their special areas of interest. Their published catalogs are leading bibliographical resources for scholars. Many of these libraries are open to the public; some have evolved to the point where external service is more important than service to the parent agency's own staff.

Libraries with extensive collections of scientific and technical literature are frequently called upon to supply materials to distant users, and many have devoted their resources especially to this purpose. The British Library maintains a Document Supply Centre at Boston Spa in Yorkshire. In a building that resembles an immense warehouse more than a conventional library, over a hundred miles of shelving house a collection of three million books and a quarter-million serial titles, as well as nearly four million technical reports on microfilm. There is hardly any accommodation for readers or borrowers at Boston Spa. Instead customers throughout the world use the post, facsimile, or electronic mail to request books on loan or photocopies of journal articles. The entire operation of the British Library Document Supply Centre is geared to the efficient fulfillment of requests from distant users. Even in a country as rich in library resources as the United States, many users find the BLDSC to be the fastest, cheapest, and surest way of obtaining the publications they need.

◆   ◆   ◆

If scientific and technical information is valuable during peacetime, it is essential in time of war. World War II was won by the application of new technology. The successful development of the atomic bomb depended upon the acquisition and application of scientific literature—from both allied and enemy sources.

When the war broke out, Germany, Britain, and the United States all developed programs to collect technical publications from enemy countries. Though at first much of this could be done openly in neutral nations (whose booksellers happily sold books and journals to all comers), as the war progressed the collection of enemy literature became increasingly an undercover operation. Intelligence services recruited librarians and documentation specialists to coordinate the gathering and distribution of technical literature. They employed the new technology of microfilm both to conceal the effort and to move extensive amounts of material by air. Speed was not the only consideration; hard-won literature shipped by sea might be lost in a submarine attack. Many of these publications were then reprinted for distribution to libraries supporting the war effort.

Though both sides tried to prevent enemy scientists from gaining useful information, both the Allies and the Axis powers were able to speed development of military technology by using information published openly in foreign journals and patents. The availability of German scientific papers on nuclear fission experiments helped to make the American atom bomb a reality in 1945. And the unsuccessful German attempt to develop a nuclear weapon relied upon information published in *Reviews of Modern Physics* and *Physical Review*. In 1944, a German submarine landed two agents and a microfilm camera on the Maine coast. They were apprehended by the Federal Bureau of Investigation before they could accomplish their mission of photographing scientific journals at the New York Public Library.

After the war, the American and British governments set up programs to collect, classify, and use captured enemy technical documents. The needs of these programs led to many of the pioneering developments that have shaped bibliography and librarianship today.

· 12 ·

The Library of the Future

What is the future of the library? Will the spread of computers and telecommunications make the book—and the library—obsolete? Will the library survive as a sort of museum, safeguarding and exhibiting printed works of art for visitors to admire but not read? Or will it flourish, as the gateway to an invisible empire of information resources?

There is no single answer to these questions. The libraries of the past played many different roles, depending on the needs of the societies in which they existed. In the future, too, libraries will have a variety of jobs to do.

One of the tasks of the library of the future will be the preservation of material whose original form is too fragile to survive. The poor quality of the paper on which many 19th- and 20th-century books and manuscripts were produced has caused a crisis for the libraries that own them. The pages of many books may crumble at even the most careful reader's touch. Despite the most stringent environmental safeguards, many volumes face certain disintegration.

Microfilm may offer the most reliable form of preservation. High-quality microfilm can last for decades, and there is no reason to suppose that it cannot last indefinitely. While modern technology makes it possible to store bulky, fragile, or valuable publications in digital form, there are dangers in relying upon it. Both the machinery used to convert printed publications to machine-readable form and the media on which the resulting electronic data are stored rapidly become obsolete. The software that interprets the electronic data is also subject to rapid change. And librarians have no experience by which to judge the permanence of electronic data. Words written on paper, parchment, or papyrus five hundred, a thousand years ago, and more, can still be read in their original form today. But we have no sure way of knowing whether a diskette or compact disc produced today will be intelligible in ten years' time.

The Internet has vastly increased the opportunities for scholarly communication and a wide range of other activities. It has made an immense range of specialized databases available to users worldwide, regardless of geographical location, often at no cost to the user. Increasingly this wealth of publication has made access to information, rather than ownership of documents, the key to the success of many libraries.

But if access is substituted for ownership, publishers will sell fewer books and subscriptions to libraries. What will be the economic incentive for continued production and publication of the literature? How will we ensure that at least one library undertakes the responsibility of acquiring, preserving, and making permanently available the content of each publication?

Libraries will continue to be responsible for maintaining the relationships with publishers that result in access to the literature needed by their patrons. And they will be responsible for ensuring that some provision is made for the permanent availability of noncurrent material. This will require some form of cooperation among libraries to provide that future needs for access to material published in the past will continue to be met.

Cataloging is an expensive process, one that lends itself to being shared among libraries. We can expect to see a continuation and expansion of the trend toward cooperative cataloging, and of the trend toward the adoption of international standards. These will increasingly reflect the capabilities and requirements of the computer, and incorporate methods taken from outside the library field.

•   •   •

As libraries opened their doors to a wider public, they began to provide patrons with some help in choosing books. Today's reference librarians are trained to help individual users select the books or other resources appropriate to their information needs. This task is even more important in the age of the Internet. It is easy and cheap to publish on the Internet, and an ever-increasing number of people, organizations, and companies do. No mechanism exists to ensure that the information appearing there is accurate. Internet users may not be able to find the reviewing media that could help them to evaluate the information they find. Even if they do, how are they to evaluate the reviewers?

This presents the library with a great opportunity. An increasing number of school and public libraries offer their patrons some form of access to the Internet, while academic and special libraries have been at the forefront of electronic access to information resources. If the library offers counsel as well as access, it will become indispensable to Internet users.

The future tasks of the national library will be the preservation of the nation's literary heritage, including its share of the common treasure of world literature, and the coordination of an increasingly extensive (and expensive!) network of intellectual resources. Governments will seldom provide enough support for these activities, so national libraries will have to use their limited resources of money, personnel, and political influence to encourage other libraries to play a role in creating and maintaining a national system.

We can expect to see an increase in scientific research on the conservation of library materials, with a special emphasis on ways of preserving large quantities cheaply. This will not just be for the benefit of historians. Scientists and doctors will often need to study observations made in the past, to understand how climates change or diseases evolve over the centuries. National libraries and library associations will also play an important part in developing physical as well as bibliographical standards for library materials.

Like the national library, the academic library of the future will have two basic missions. It will continue to provide students and teachers with access to a wide range of material for education and research. And it will train its users in the skills needed to discover, access, and evaluate information. A particular challenge to the academic library will be the provision of support to distant learners, especially to those whose primary interaction with the campus is electronic. This support will have to go well beyond making the library's collections available to students off campus. A major role of the academic library will be to play an active part in their educational experience.

More than any other type of library, the future of the special library lies in the expertise that it can bring to finding needed information, wherever it is located. As the nature of published information grows more complex, and as the stakes go higher—not knowing about regulations or patents can be very costly—this expertise will become more important. But like many other specialized services, the information needs of corporations and government agencies will increasingly be met by recourse to outside consultants rather than by permanent employees.

If the continued existence of the free public library is to be justified, it will have to be as an educational rather than a recreational institution. The public library collection will have to reflect the long-term needs of the society it supports rather than the short-term desires of people who read books for amusement. This will fit in with the increasing need that an information-based society will have for lifelong continuing education. The public library of the future, then, will in many ways represent a return to the original concept of the free library: a people's university, whose serious purpose justifies its public support. In the developing countries, where a rapidly increasing population will strain the limited resources for formal education, the public library's role as an educational agency will be even stronger.

◆　◆　◆

The future will certainly bring substantial changes in the ways in which information is produced, transmitted, and preserved. The continuing advance of computer technology will increase access to information. But paradoxically it will also increase the importance of such traditional library functions as cataloging and reader guidance.

The functions of the librarian have always been to select the material that his or her constituents will require; to catalog it so that those who would use it can know what is available and where it is kept; and to preserve it for both contemporary readers and those who will follow. With the opening of libraries to a wider public, another task fell to the librarian, that of helping patrons choose the library materials most appropriate to their needs.

None of these tasks will disappear with the emergence of the electronic library. Somebody will have to perform them: if not the librarian, then his or her replacement. So long as people continue to use the knowledge they have inherited from their ancestors and learned from their contemporaries, so long as human ingenuity and creativity increase the store of information, there will be a need for persons and institutions to collect, to catalog, to preserve, and to guide. Books, and libraries, have changed over the thousands of years since the invention of writing. The pace of change accelerated with the invention of printing, and again in the age of the computer. But the essential task of the librarian has remained the same: to collect and preserve the record of human accomplishment and imagination, and to put this record in the hands of those who would use it.

Notes

1. "The Instruction for Merikare," in Miriam Lichtheim, ed., *Ancient Egyptian Literature: A Book of Readings* (Berkeley: University of California Press, 1973-1980), 1:97 ff.

2. Assurbanipal, quoted in N.K. Sandars, ed., *The Epic of Gilgamesh*, rev. ed. (Baltimore: Penguin Books, 1964), 8.

3. Ecclesiastes 12:12.

4. Deuteronomy 31: 26.

5. I Samuel 10:25.

6. Cicero, *Ad Atticus* 4.8.2, trans. E. O. Winstedt (Loeb Classical Library).

7. Seneca, *De Tranquillitate Animi* 9.4-7, trans. John W. Basore (Loeb Classical Library, *Moral Essays*).

8. Karl Christ, *The Handbook of Medieval Library History*, ed. and trans. Theophil M. Otto (Metuchen, N.J.: Scarecrow Press, 1984), 64-65.

9. *Vita S. Galli*, cap. 12, quoted in James Midgley Clark, *The Abbey of St. Gall as a Center of Literature and Art* (Cambridge: Cambridge University Press, 1926), 27.

10. Quoted in Lucy Menzies, *Columba of Iona: A Study of His Life, His Times, and His Influence* (London: Dent, 1920), 25.

11. Bede, quoted in Eleanor Shipley Duckett, *Anglo-Saxon Saints and Scholars* (New York: Macmillan, 1947), 276.

12. Einhart, *Vita Karoli Magni*, ch. 33, quoted in Christ, *Handbook of Medieval Library History*, 122.

13. Charlemagne, *Karoli Epistola de Litteris Colendis*, quoted in Eleanor Shipley Duckett, *Alcuin: Friend of Charlemagne: His World and His Work* (New York: Macmillan, 1951), 125.

14. Eadbeorht, epilogue to the St. Gall Codex of the *Collectio Canonum Hibernensis*, quoted in Clark, *The Abbey of St. Gall*, 62-63.

15. *Rule of St. Benedict*, ch. 48, in Timothy Fry, ed., *RB 1980: The Rule of St. Benedict in Latin and English with Notes* (Collegeville, Minnesota: Liturgical Press, 1981).

16. Abridged from Hildemar, *Expositio Hildemari*, ch. 48, in Walter Horn and Ernest Born, *The Plan of St. Gall: A Study of the Architecture and Economy of, and Life in a Paradigmatic Carolingian Monastery* (Berkeley: University of California Press, 1979), 1: 149.

17. Quoted in François Dolbeau, "Les usagers des bibliothèques," 401, in *Histoire des bibliothèques françaises,* ed. André Vernet (Paris: Promodis, 1988-91), 1: 395-413.

18. David McMullen, *State and Scholars in T'ang China* (Cambridge: Cambridge University Press, 1988), 9 (paraphrasing *Thung Chien Kang Mu,* ch. 3, p. 46b).

19. Quoted in Edwin O. Reischauer and John K. Fairbank. *East Asia: The Great Tradition* (Boston: Houghton Mifflin, 1960), 382.

20. Thomas Watters, *On Yuan Chwang's Travels in India,* A.D. *629–645* (London: Royal Asiatic Society, 1904-1905), 1: 386.

21. Al-Mutannabi, *Diwan*, quoted in Olga Pinto, "The Libraries of the Arabs during the Time of the Abbasides," trans. F. Krenkow, *Pakistan Library Review* 2(1-2): 46 (March 1959).

22. Al-Makrizi, *Khitat*, 1: 458, quoted in Pinto, "The Libraries of the Arabs," 59.

23. Ibn Hayyan, quoted in Pinto, "The Libraries of the Arabs," 67.

24. Quoted in Ladislaus Buzás, *German Library History, 800-1945*, trans. William D. Boyd (Jefferson, N.C.: McFarland, 1986), 200.

25. Quoted in L.M. Newman, *Leibniz (1646-1716) and the German Library Scene* (London: Library Association, 1966), 47.

26. Vespasiano da Bisticci, *The Vespasiano Memoirs: Lives of Illustrious Men of the XVth Century*, trans. William George and Emily Waters (London: Routledge, 1926), 104.

27. Quoted in James Dennistoun "of Dennistoun," *Memoirs of the Dukes of Urbino, Illustrating the Arms, Arts and Literature of Italy, 1440-1630*, ed. Edward Hutton (London: John Lane, 1909), 1: 241-43.

28. Quoted in Edward Edwards, *Free Town Libraries, Their Formation, Management, and History, in Britain, France, Germany, and America, Together with Brief Notices of Book-Collectors, and of Their Respective Places of Deposit of Their Surviving Collections* (London: Trübner, 1869), 262.

29. Sixtus IV, *Ad decorem militantis Ecclesiae*, quoted in Theodore Wesley Koch, "The Vatican Library: An Historical Sketch," in *The Vatican Library: Two Papers* (Jersey City: Snead & Co., 1929), 13.

30. Gabriel Naudé, *Instructions concerning erecting of a library, presented to My Lord the President de Mesme; and now interpreted by Jo. Evelyn* (Cambridge, Massachusetts: Printed for Houghton Mifflin at the Riverside Press, 1903), 33. [reprint of 1661 edition]

31. Martin Luther, "To the Councilmen of All Cities in Germany that They Establish and Maintain Christian Schools," trans. Albert T.W. Steinhaeuser, in *The Christian in Society, II*, ed. Walter I. Brandt (Vol. 45 of *Luther's Works*, American ed. Philadelphia: Muhlenberg Press, 1962), 373.

32. Luther, "To the Councilmen of All Cities in Germany," 375

33. John Bale, *Laboryouse Journey of John Leylande*, leaf B1 recto, quoted in J.C.T. Oates, *Cambridge University Library: A History from the Beginnings to the Copyright Act of Queen Anne* (Cambridge: Cambridge University Press, 1986), 77.

34. Quoted in John Edwin Pomfret, *The Henry E. Huntington Library and Art Gallery, from Its Beginnings to 1969* (San Marino, Calif.: Huntington Library, 1969), 13.

35. Edward Edwards, *Memoirs of Libraries, Including a Handbook of Library Economy* (London: Trübner, 1859), 2: 277.

36. Quoted in Edward Miller, *Prince of Librarians: The Life and Times of Antonio Panizzi of the British Museum* (Athens: Ohio University Press, 1967), 275.

37. Paraphrased in Arundell Esdaile, *National Libraries of the World: Their History, Administration and Public Services*, 2d ed., rev. by F.J. Hill (London: Library Association, 1957), 14.

38. Thackeray to Antonio Panizzi, 10 March 1850, in *The Letters and Private Papers of William Makepeace Thackeray*, ed. Gordon N. Ray (Cambridge: Harvard University Press, 1945-1946), 2: 651.

39. J. G. Kohl, *Russia and the Russians in 1842* (London, 1842), 1: 290, quoted in Mary Stuart, *Aristocrat-Librarian in Service to the Tsar: Aleksei Nikolaevich Olenin and the Imperial Public Library* (Bouder, Colo.: East European Monographs, 1956), 135.

40. Jefferson, quoted in Charles A. Goodrum and Helen W. Dalrymple, *The Library of Congress*, 2d ed. (Boulder, Colo.: Westview Press, 1982), 14.

41. Quoted in Hugo Kunoff, *The Foundations of the German Academic Library* (Chicago: American Library Association, 1982), 142.

42. *Catalogue of Books in the Library of the College of New Jersey*, January 29, 1760, quoted in Louis Shores, *Origins of the American College Library, 1638-1800* (Nashville: George Peabody College, 1934), 29-30.

43. Herbert B. Adams, "Seminar Libraries and University Extension," *Johns Hopkins University Studies in Historical and Political Science*, 5th ser.,

12: 10-11 (1887), quoted in Lawrence Thompson, "The Historical Background of Departmental and Collegiate Libraries," *Library Quarterly* 12(1): 49-74 (January 1942), 60-61.

44. Alban Dumas, "Des bibliothèques des facultés aux bibliothèques universitaires," 427, in *Histoire des bibliothèques françaises,* ed. André Vernet (Paris: Promodis, 1988-1991), 3: 417-34.

45. Robert Talmadge, "Farmington Plan Survey," *College and Research Libraries* 19: 376 (1958), quoted in Arthur T. Hamlin, *The University Library in the United States: Its Origins and Development* (Philadelphia: University of Pennsylvania Press, 1981), 193.

46. Quoted in Walter Muir Whitehill, *Boston Public Library: A Centennial History* (Cambridge: Harvard University Press, 1956), 81.

47. Leon Carnovsky, "The Public Libraries of Paris," *Library Quarterly* 22(3): 194-99 (July 1952), 196.

48. Quoted in George Chandler, *Libraries, Documentation and Bibliography in the USSR 1917-1971: Survey and Critical Analysis of Soviet Studies 1967-1971* (London: Seminar Press, 1972), 23.

49. Quoted in Chandler, *Libraries, Documentation and Bibliography in the USSR,* 16.

50. Lenin, *Complete Collected Works,* 44: 422, quoted in Simon Francis, ed., *Libraries in the USSR* (London: Clive Bingley, 1971), 40.

51. George Ticknor, quoted in Whitehill, *Boston Public Library*, 33.

52. V. Petroshan, quoted in Axel Andersen, J. B. Friis-Hansen, and Leif Kajberg, *Libraries and Information Centres in the Soviet Union* (Ballerup, Denmark: Bibliotekscentralens, 1985), 47.

53. A. Chabisova, quoted in Andersen et al., *Libraries and Information Centres in the Soviet Union*, 47.

54. Quoted in Wyndham D. Miles, *A History of the National Library of Medicine: The Nation's Treasury of Medical Knowledge* (Bethesda, Md.: National Library of Medicine, 1982), 131.

Glossary

abbey: the building or settlement housing a community of monks; another term for monastery

abbot: the head of a monastery

abstract: a brief summary of a journal article or technical report intended to tell the reader enough to decide whether to read the entire publication

Allies: the group of countries, including the United States, Great Britain, and the Soviet Union, that won World War II

archive: a collection of documents recording the everyday activities of a company or organization

Ark of the Covenant: the wooden container, kept in the Temple in Jerusalem, in which the Divine Presence was considered to reside

Assyria: the ancient empire that flourished in the upper Tigris valley (in present-day Iraq) during the 9th and 8th centuries B.C.E.

Axis: the group of countries, including Germany, Japan, and Italy, that lost World War II

Babylon: an ancient city in the lower Euphrates valley (in present-day Iraq) whose empire overthrew the Assyrians in 612 B.C.E.; among the peoples it conquered were the Jews, who were deported from Palestine to Babylon in 587 B.C.E.

bibliography: the study of books; the word is often used in the narrower sense of a list of books

bibliophile: a lover of books

caliph: the ruler of a Muslim state

calligraphy: fine handwriting

canon: a collection of books recognized by a church or religious authority, such as the books accepted as parts of the Bible

canon law: the code of laws governing the Roman Catholic church

Christendom: that part of the world inhabited by Christians

church council: a meeting of church leaders to decide important issues concerning the beliefs, practices, and organization of the Catholic church

Church Fathers: early Christian writers whose teachings are considered authoritative by the Catholic church

civil law: the legal system of most European and Latin American countries, derived from that of the Roman empire, in which legislative bodies are the most important source of law

codex: the book as we know it today, consisting of leaves of paper gathered between protective covers and attached to them

collate: to examine a copy of a book or manuscript and compare its contents with another copy

colonnade: a series of columns placed at regular intervals

common law: the legal system of English-speaking countries, evolved from the customary law of England

courtier: a person of high rank or social status who forms part of a ruler's household

cuneiform: a system of writing using wedge-shaped characters impressed into wet clay with reed instruments

curriculum: the course of study in an educational institution

Dark Ages: the period between the downfall of the Western Roman empire during the 5th century C.E. and the revival of commerce and learning in the 10th century

Dead Sea Scrolls: a collection of writings produced by a Jewish sect called the Essenes in the 1st century B.C.E. and hidden in a cave at Qumran until their rediscovery in 1947

dissertation: a report, usually the length of a book, of a piece of original research carried out in the course of earning a doctoral degree from a university

documentation: the study of scientific communication and the publications resulting from scientific activity

dynasty: a succession of rulers from the same family

etymology: the study of the origins of words

excommunicate: to declare that a person is no longer a member of a church or congregation

Fertile Crescent: the lands stretching from the Persian Gulf to the Nile valley in which agriculture, writing, and civilization first arose

folio: a sheet of paper folded once, or a book whose pages are of the large size produced by folding the paper only once before sewing them together

genealogy: the study of family history

humanism: a cultural movement at the time of the Renaissance, inspired by Greek and Roman art and literature, that emphasized the capabilities and achievements of humans over religious concerns

humanistic: concerned with classical art and literature rather than with theology

imprint: a statement naming the publisher of a book and the date and place of publication

interlibrary loan: the loan of books or other materials by one library to another

Jesuit: a member of the Society of Jesus, a Roman Catholic order founded by Ignatius Loyola in 1534 and known for its missionary and educational work

jurisprudence: the science of law

Koran: the sacred book of Islam, containing the word of God as revealed to his prophet Muhammad

lectern: a table with a sloping surface, upon which a reader could rest the book he or she was reading

Lent: the forty weekdays before Easter, observed by Christians as a period of prayer and penitence

literary heritage: a collective term for the literature produced throughout its history by members of a group of people, such as a nation or a religious group

liturgy: the system of prayers and rituals established by a religious body to govern public worship

Medes: a ancient people who lived in western Persia (present-day Iran); they conquered Assyria but were later incorporated into the Persian Empire

Mesopotamia: the land between the Tigris and Euphrates rivers, in present-day Iraq

microfilm: photographic film used to record miniature images of printed pages, to save space, to preserve material in danger of deterioration, or to produce cheap copies of rare or bulky material

miniaturist: someone who paints small pictures as decorations or illustrations in books

monastery: the building or settlement housing a community of monks

monk: a person who lives as part of a religious community under its rules of discipline

octavo: a sheet of paper folded four times to make eight pages, or a book whose pages are of the size produced by folding the paper this way (this book is in octavo size, although modern production methods do not necessarily use traditional sizes of paper)

online public-access catalog: a library catalog produced in the form of a computer database that library patrons may search for themselves

pagan: a person who does not adhere to Judaism, Christianity, or Islam; in the early years of Christianity, the term was used to refer to one who followed the traditional religion of the Roman empire

papyrus: a writing surface made from the stem of a common reed, *Cyperus papyrus*, that grows in southern Europe and northern Africa

parchment: the skin of a sheep, cleaned and treated for use as a writing surface

patristic: pertaining to the Church Fathers

Pergamene Library: the library established in Pergamon, a city in Asia Minor (i.e., modern Turkey), by its Attalid rulers in the 3rd century B.C.E.

philology: the study of the history and development of languages

precedent: the decision of a court in one case that is considered to apply to any later cases of a similar nature

psalter: a book containing the Psalms of David from the Bible

public good: something that benefits society as a whole, for which it is impossible or impractical to require individual users to pay the cost of producing or maintaining it

rag paper: paper made by grinding cotton or linen cloth to a pulp

Reformation: the 16th-century process of reforming Christian belief and practice, which led to the formation of Protestant churches

Renaissance: the revival of learning, inspired by Roman art and literature, that began in 14th-century Italy and spread across Europe in the 14th through 16th centuries

research library: a library whose collections are intended for the use of researchers and serious students rather than for the provision of entertainment or immediately practical information

saint: a man or woman declared by a church to be an example of holiness and (in some churches) to have the power to intercede with God on behalf of ordinary people

Serapeum: the temple of Serapis in Alexandria, whose library was affiliated with that of the Museion (scholars are unsure of the exact nature of this relationship)

statute: a law enacted by a legislative body

stele: a stone column with writing or pictures carved into its surface

syllabary: list of written characters that represent the syllables of a language

tabernacle: the portable building used as the center of Jewish worship before the construction of the Temple in Jerusalem

thesis: a report of research carried out in the course of earning a degree from a university (some writers use "thesis" as a synonym for "dissertation," while other use it specifically to describe research performed for the master's degree)

Torah: the biblical books of Genesis, Exodus, Leviticus, Numbers, and Deuteronomy ("the five books of Moses"), which constitute the most sacred of the Jewish Scriptures, inscribed on a parchment scroll

union catalog: a listing of the books owned by the members of a group of libraries

Vatican: the headquarters of the Roman Catholic church

vellum: the skin of a calf, cleaned and treated for use as a writing surface

vernacular: the language spoken by the ordinary people, as distinguished from learned languages (such as Latin) used only by an educated minority

vizier: an Arabic term for a high-ranking officer in the government who was usually second in power only to the ruler

wood-pulp paper: paper made from ground-up wood treated with chemicals, rather than from cotton or linen fibers

Suggestions for Further Reading

A more detailed history of libraries may be found in my book *The Story of Libraries: From the Invention of Writing to the Computer Age* (New York: Continuum, 1998). That book contains an extensive bibliography; the suggestions presented here are limited to a few basic titles.

History of Books and Printing

Avrin, Leila. *Scribes, Script, and Books: The Book Arts from Antiquity to the Renaissance*. Chicago: American Library Association, 1991. Traces the development of written communication from the first cave paintings to the invention of the printing press, with considerable attention to the crafts of papermaking, calligraphy, and bookbinding.

Olmert, Michael. *The Smithsonian Book of Books*. Washington: Smithsonian Books, 1992. A broad-ranging historical survey of all aspects of the book arts, illustrated with beautiful color photographs of books and book making.

Steinberg, S. H. *Five Hundred Years of Printing*. New ed., revised by John Trevitt. London: The British Library; New Castle, Delaware: Oak Knoll Press, 1996. An updated edition of the classic book on the history of printing and its effects on literature and society. Extensive illustrations trace the development of printing as both an art and a technology.

Vervliet, Hendrik, D. L., ed. *The Book through Five Thousand Years: A Survey.* London and New York: Phaidon, 1972. An enormous survey whose four sections cover the prehistory of books and writing, the book in the Orient, the manuscript in the West, and the printed book in the West. Each chapter is written by a specialist in its subject and accompanied by photographs, many in color.

History of Libraries

Cole, John Y. *Jefferson's Legacy: A Brief History of the Library of Congress.* Washington: Library of Congress, 1993. An account of the origins, collections, and activities of the greatest American library.

Dickson, Paul. *The Library in America: A Celebration in Words and Pictures.* New York: Facts on File, 1986. A collection of personal narratives, documents, drawings, and photographs showing the role that libraries have played in the lives of Americans since colonial days.

Encyclopedia of Library and Information Science. New York: Marcel Dekker, 1968–. A multivolume collection of articles on all aspects of libraries and librarianship, including all geographical regions and historical periods.

Hobson, Anthony. *Great Libraries.* New York: Putnam, 1970. A large-format, lavishly illustrated tribute to thirty-three of the Western world's great libraries and their collections.

Wiegand, Wayne A., and Donald G. Davis, eds. *Encyclopedia of Library History.* New York: Garland, 1994. A one-volume survey of the major people, institutions, and themes in library history.

Timeline

Chapter 1: The Fertile Crescent

ca. -3000	Sumerians invent writing
ca. -2725	Weshptah (Egyptian vizier) suffers stroke, physicians consult "case of writings"
ca. -2500	Ebla archives
-2250	Ebla destroyed by Assyrians
-1810 to -1760	Palace archive at Mari
ca. -1700	*Book of Surgery* (Egypt)
-1650 to -1200	Hittite state flourishes, with Bogazkoy (Hattusha) as its capital
-13th c.	Ramesses II establishes Ramesseum
-11th c.	Samuel records rules of Israelite monarchy
-8th c.	Temple of Nabu founded in Nineveh
-7th c.	Book of Deuteronomy
-668 to -627	Reign of Assurbanipal
-612	fall of Nineveh
-6th c.	Israelites exiled to Babylonia
ca. -100	Dead Sea Scrolls written
+2 c.	canonization process of Hebrew scriptures completed

Chapter 2: Greece and Rome

-9th c.	Homeric period
-4th c.	Alexandria founded
-3rd c.	Pergamene library founded
-246 to -221	reign of Ptolemy III
-168	Crates of Mallos sent to Rome
-106 to -43	lifetime of Cicero
-48	Fire destroys 400,000 books at Alexandria during Caesar's Alexandran War
-40 to +14	Reign of Augustus
-4 to +65	lifetime of Seneca
-31	Rome becomes an empire
+4th c.	Codex begins to replace roll in Western libraries
+641	Arabs under 'Amr ibn al-'As invade Egypt

Chapter 3: Medieval Europe

313	Emperor Constantine makes Christianity the state religion of Rome
432	Patrick brings Christianity to Ireland
6th c.	Monte Cassino founded
521	Columba (Columcille) born
563	Columba founds monastery at Iona
673 to 735	lifetime of Bede
710	Arab conquest of Spain begins (lasts until 1492)
ca. 735	Egbert founds cathedral school of York
771 to 814	Reign of Charles the Great (Charlemagne)

782	Alcuin meets Charlemagne
8th-9th c.	Northmen ravage Ireland
9th c.	*Plan of St. Gall* sets forth design for ideal Benedictine monastery
926	St. Gall library moved to Reichenau
12th c.	students and teachers gather in Bologna and Paris
ca. 1167	University of Oxford founded
1200	University of Paris receives royal patent
1257	Sorbonne founded at University of Paris

Chapter 4: China and India

China

-1122 to -256	Chou dynasty
-551 to -479	lifetime of K'ung fu-tzu (Confucius)
-221 to -207	Ch'in dynasty
-212	"burning of the books"
-206 to +220	Han dynasty
-2nd c.	paper invented
+1st c.	paper first used for writing
159	Imperial Library formally established
175 to 183	Five Classics and Analects carved on stone steles
3rd c.	Imperial Library copies bamboo books onto paper
220 to 589	Six Dynasties period of disunity
265 to 304	Chin dynasty
581 to 618	Sui dynasty
618 to 907	T'ang dynasty

622	Capital moved from Lo-yang to Ch'ang-an
1035	Tun-Huang caves sealed up
1368 to 1644	Ming dynasty
1644 to 1912	Ch'ing dynasty
1736-1795	Ch'ien-lung
1782	"Complete Library of the Four Treasures" finished

India

-6th c.	Rise of Buddhism and Jainism
+5th c.	Jetavana monastery in its prime
629 to 645	Hsuan-Tsang makes pilgrimage to India, visits Nalanda monastery

Chapter 5: The Islamic World

ca. 610 to 630	Muhammad receives the Koran
622	Hegira (Muhammad's flight to Medina, marking beginning of Islamic era)
710	Muslim invasion of Spain
751	art of papermaking reaches the Islamic world at Samarkand
ca. 830	Caliph al-Ma'mun founds *Bayt al-hikma* at Baghdad
ca. 900	Ibn Hamdan founds *dar-al'ilm* at Mosul
929 to 1031	Umayyid dynasty in Spain
10th c.	Royal library flourishes at Córdoba
988	Al-Nadim publishes *Fihrist al'ulum*
ca. 996	Sabur ibn Ardasir founds *dar-al'ilm* at Baghdad

1004	*Dar al-hikma* at Cairo
1096 to 1291	Crusades
1175	Saladin conquers Egypt
13th c.	lifetime of Ibn Hayyan
1258	Mongols destroy Baghdad
1259	Mongol leader Hulagu builds observatory and library at Maraghah
1492	Christian reconquest of Spain completed
1499	80,000 Muslim books burnt in Granada

Chapter 6: The Printed Book

1363 to 1447	lifetime of Niccolo de' Nicoli
1389 to 1464	lifetime of Cosimo de' Medici
1398 to 1455	lifetime of Tommaso Parentucelli
1422 to 1482	lifetime of Federigo da Montefeltro, Duke of Urbino
1444	library of San Marco founded in Florence
1444	Duke Humfrey of Gloucester gives books for a library at Oxford University
1447	Tomasso becomes Pope Nicholas V
1448 to 1492	lifetime of Lorenzo de' Medici
1450	Bibliotèca Vaticana founded
1452	Gutenberg issues first printed Bible
1453	Constantinople falls to the Turks
1483 to 1546	lifetime of Martin Luther
1489 to 1492	John Lascaris visits Constantinople and the East in search of Greek manuscripts
1521 to 1597	lifetime of Peter Canisius
1531	English Reformation begins
1545 to 1613	lifetime of Thomas Bodley
1550	Royal commissioners visit Oxford, destroy

	Duke Humfrey's library
1571	Bibliotheca Laurentiana founded in Florence
1598	Thomas Bodley reestablishes "public library" at Oxford University
1600 to 1653	lifetime of Gabriel Naudé
1646 to 1716	lifetime of Gottfried Wilhelm Leibniz
1658	Urbino books incorporated into Vatican Library

Chapter 7: Kings and Congressmen

14th c.	reign of Charles V
1735	Bibliothèque du Roi permanently opened to public
1753	death of Hans Sloane
1759	British Museum opens to public
1774	Continental Congress assembles in Philadelphia
1788 to 1789	French Revolution
1797 to 1879	lifetime of Antonio Panizzi
1800	Congressional library established at Washington
1803 to 1815	Napoleonic wars
1815	Napoleon defeated at Waterloo
1815	Congress buys Jefferson's library
1837	Panizzi appointed Keeper of Printed Books, British Museum
1837 to 1913	lifetime of John Pierpont Morgan
1850 to 1927	lifetime of Henry Edwards Huntington
1861 to 1865	American Civil War
1914	Congressional Research Service created at

	Library of Congress
1924	Morgan Library opened to public
1928	Huntington Library opened

Chapter 8: Colleges and Universities

1350 to 1600	Renaissance
1473 to 1543	lifetime of Copernicus
16th c.	Reformation
1547 to 1616	lifetime of Cervantes
1564 to 1616	lifetime of Shakespeare
1564 to 1642	lifetime of Galileo
1578 to 1657	lifetime of William Harvey
1622 to 1673	lifetime of Molière
1636	Harvard College founded at Cambridge, Massachusetts
1642 to 1727	lifetime of Isaac Newton
1737	University of Göttingen opens in northern Germany
1763 to 1812	Christian Gottlob Heyne serves as chief librarian at Göttingen
ca. 1800	seminar introduced to German universities
1861	Yale University grants first American Ph.D. degree
1914 to 1918	World War I
1939 to 1945	World War II
1951	Midwest Inter-Library Center established

Chapter 9: The People's Libraries

1731	Benjamin Franklin organizes Library

	Company of Philadelphia
1835 to 1919	lifetime of Andrew Carnegie
1842	Mudie's Select Library begins operation
1850	Public Libraries Act becomes law in Great Britain
1854	Boston Public Library opens
1876	Dewey Decimal System published
1876	American Library Association founded
1879	New York Free Circulating Library opens
1886	Andrew Carnegie begins giving money for library construction
1917	Russian Revolution
1930s	Nazi regime expands public libraries in Germany
1939	American Library Association proclaims "Library Bill of Rights"

Chapter 10: Libraries for Young People

ca. 1890	first American public library children's room opens
1900	first school librarian appointed
1924	L'Heure Joyeuse opens in Paris
1957	*Sputnik*, the first artificial earth satellite, launched by USSR
1958	National Defense Education Act

Chapter 11: Libraries at Work

-21st c.	Hammurabi proclaims laws of Babylon

-460 to -377	lifetime of Hippocrates
+130 to +200	lifetime of Galen
16th c.	"Reception" of Roman law by countries of continental Europe
1838 to 1913	lifetime of John Shaw Billings
1854	Patent Office Library opened to the public in London
1865	John Shaw Billings placed in charge of Surgeon-General's library
1879	*Index Medicus* begins publication
1880	*Index-Catalogue of the Library of the Surgeon-General's Office* first published
1945	atomic bombs used at Hiroshima and Nagasaki
1956	Surgeon-General's Library placed under civilian management, renamed National Library of Medicine
1967	National Library of Medicine offers experimental online access to MEDLINE
1972	British Museum Library becomes part of new British Library

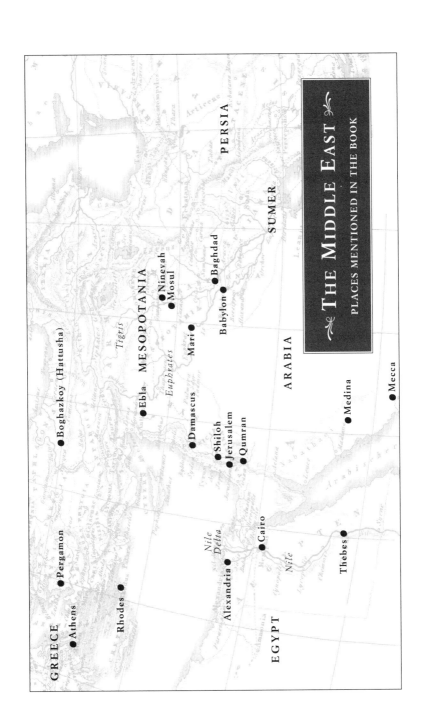

THE MIDDLE EAST

PLACES MENTIONED IN THE BOOK

GREECE

Athens

Pergamon

Rhodes

Boghazkoy (Hattusha)

MESOPOTANIA

Tigris

Euphrates

Ebla

Damascus

Mari

Ninevah

Mosul

Babylon

Baghdad

SUMER

PERSIA

Shiloh

Jerusalem

Qumran

ARABIA

Medina

Mecca

Alexandria

Nile
Delta

Cairo

Nile

Thebes

EGYPT

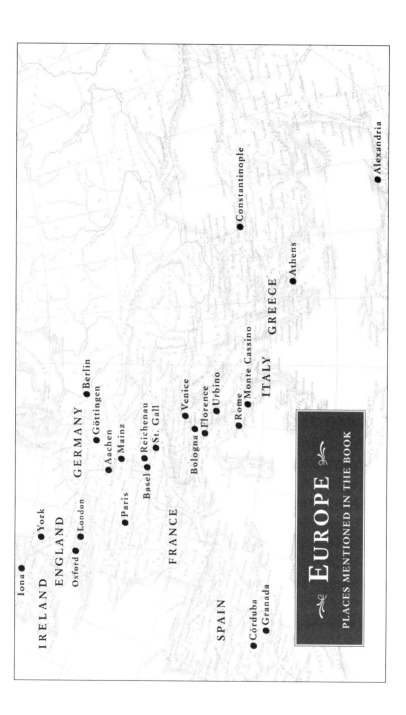

EUROPE

PLACES MENTIONED IN THE BOOK

Index

Panizzi, Antonio, 77-78, plate 12
papal libraries, 69-70
paper, 38, 42-43, 45, 58, 81, 122
papyrus, 15, 26-27, 58
parchment, 26-27, 31, 33, 38, 43, 58
Paris, 35, 70, 104; Bibliothèque
    Nationale, 76-80; l'Heure Joyeuse,
    110; Sorbonne, 37-38, plate 5;
    University of Paris, 35
patents, 119
patent office libraries, 119
patristic literature, 33, 36, 66, 69
Pergamon, 23, 24
periodicals, 97, 98, 116, 120, 121;
    indexes, 116-17, 119
Persian literature, 58
Petrograd, *see* Saint Petersburg
Philadelphia, 78, 98
philanthropy, 61-62, 74-75, 100, 101
picture books, 109
pilgrims, 28, 47
Plan of St Gall, plate 3
poplar bark, 58
preservation of library materials, 81,
    122-23, 124-25
Princeton University, 84
printing: effect of, 66-67, 72, 74; move-
    able type, 66; spread of, 66; wood
    block, 45, 46
private libraries: in antiquity, 25; in the
    Orient, 44-45; in the Islamic world,
    59, 61; in medieval Europe, 34; in
    the Renaissance, 67-69, 70-71; in
    modern times, 74-75, 98
professional societies, 118-19
Protestantism, 67, 71-72, 97
Ptolemy III Euergetes, king of Egypt, 21
Public Libraries Act of 1850, 99
public libraries, 97-107, 108-14; in
    antiquity, 25-26; in continental
    Europe, 103-6; educational and
    social mission, 99-101, 103, 105,
    106-7; future of, 124, 126; in Great
    Britain, 99-102; Islamic, 70, 72;
    selection policies, 100-1, 103, 104,
    106, 109, 112-13, 114; in the United
    States, 100-3, 106-7, 108-9, 111-12,
    plates 13, 15, 16, 17, 18; users,
    100-1, 102, 104, 105-6, 111-12
public schools, 100, 108, 110, 111-12
publishing, *see* book trade
puppet programs, 109

quadrivium, 36
Qumran, 19

radicalism, 103
Ramesses II, king of Egypt, 16
Ramesseum, 16
Raphael, 70
Ratnadadhi, 47
readers advisory service, 106, 110, 113,
    126-27
reading aloud, 30, 33, 36, 69, 97, 98
recreational reading, 98-99, 101, 104,
    111
Redwood Library (Newport, R.I.), 98
reference collections, 101-2
reference service, 103
Reformation, 67, 82, 97
Reichenau, 35
Religious Tract Society, 99
Renaissance, 58, 67-70, 82
rental libraries, 97-99
reviewing, 124
Rhodes, 21
Rome, 23, 24-26; Imperial Library, 35;
    Palatine Library, 34; Vatican Library,
    69-70, 74, plate 8
royal libraries, 75-77, 78
rubrication, 33
Rule of St. Benedict, 28, 32
Russia, 78, 104-5, 110

Sabur ibn Ardasir, 59-60
Saint Gall, 32, 35, plate 3
Saint Petersburg (Russia), 104; Imperial
    Library, 78
saints' lives, 33
Saladin, sultan of Egypt and Syria, 64
San Marco (Florence), 68
Saracens, 35
school libraries, 71-72, 110, 111-12, 124
scientific literature, 16, 17, 58, 59, 82,
    100-1, 119-21
scribes, 13, 15, 17, 31-32, 60-61, 62, 63,
    plate 4
scriptorium, 31-32, plates 3, 4
self-improvement, 100, 111, 126
seminar libraries, 85-86
Seneca, 25
serials, *see* periodicals
settlement houses, plate 18
Sixtus IV, pope, 70
Sloane, Hans, 77